Essential Stitc

GOLDWORK

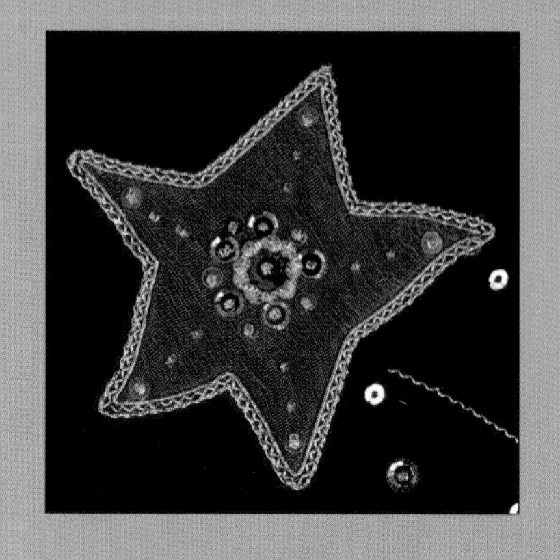

Essential Stitch Guide

GOLDWORK

HELEN McCOOK

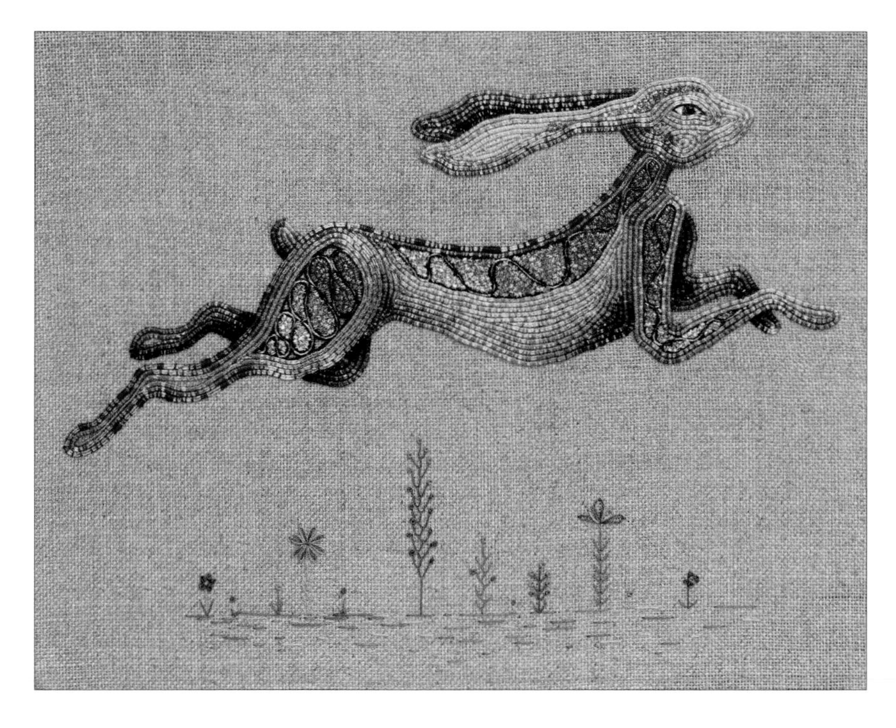

SEARCH PRESS

First published in Great Britain 2012
Search Press Limited
Wellwood, North Farm Road,
Tunbridge Wells, Kent TN2 3DR

ISBN: 978-1-84448-702-8

SUPPLIERS
If you have any difficulty obtaining any of the materials and equipment mentioned in this book, please visit the Search Press website: www.searchpress.com

For more details about the work of the Royal School of Needlework, including courses, tours, our Studio, tutors and where some of our work can be seen, please go to our website: www.royal-needlework.org.uk

Printed in China

Page 1
Indian Summer
Helen McCook
Gilt metal threads, coloured twist, sequins, beads and appliqué to silk dupion ground.

Page 2
Three Wishes** **(details)
Helen McCook
Silver metal threads, spangles, crystals and appliqué to velvet ground.

Page 3
Fearless Freedom
Helen McCook
Japanese thread, copper, gilt and silver bright check thread, and assorted stranded cotton threads to linen ground.

CONTENTS

The Royal School of Needlework

The Royal School of Needlework was founded in 1872 by Lady Victoria Welby because she wanted to ensure that the arts and techniques of high-quality hand embroidery were kept alive. At the time, Berlin wool work, a form of canvaswork, was all the rage, almost to the exclusion of all other techniques. The RSN began to train people in the wide range of historic techniques from blackwork to silk shading and from metal thread work to whitework. Working with designers such as William Morris, Walter Crane and Edward Burne-Jones, they created pieces for exhibitions in the US and Paris, and for private commissions.

Since then, the RSN has used these techniques to make new works for a wide variety of organisations from cathedrals and synagogues to historic buildings and commercial organisations as well as for individuals. We have also worked for every British monarch since Queen Victoria.

Today, the RSN is at the forefront of teaching hand-embroidery techniques to the highest standard and welcomes people from all over the world on to its courses every year. We also have an extensive collection of embroidered textiles and archival material which acts as a fantastic resource for ideas and inspiration. Visitors to our rooms at Hampton Court Palace, whether for classes or tours, can see a changing range of works from the Collection on display.

While setting a high standard, the RSN exists to encourage more people to participate in hand embroidery and, to this end, runs courses from beginner level in every technique, for those who want to pursue embroidery as a leisure interest, right through to our professional Certificate, Diploma and Foundation Degree for those who want to develop their future careers in embroidered textiles. While we are trying to increase the number of locations in which courses are held, we are well aware that Hampton Court Palace, a few other UK centres and San Francisco and Tokyo are not easily accessible to many people who would

like to explore embroidery through the RSN approach, hence this series of Essential Stitch Guides.

Each book is written by an RSN Graduate Apprentice who has spent three years at the RSN learning techniques and then applying them in the RSN Studio, working on pieces from our Collection or on customers' contemporary and historic pieces. All are also tutors on our courses.

Alongside the actual stitches and historic examples of the technique you will also find a selection of works by the author and other RSN Apprentices and Students to show how a technique can really be used in new ways. While the RSN uses traditional stitch techniques as its medium, we believe that they can be used to create very contemporary works to ensure hand embroidery is not just kept alive, but flourishes into the future. We hope these images will inspire you to explore and develop your own work.

Opposite and below

Hampton Court Palace, Surrey, home of the Royal School of Needlework.

INTRODUCTION

Long before I ever held an embroidery needle and became immersed in the fine tradition that is the world of bespoke embroidery, I recognised that the beauty of metal thread work held a strong appeal for me – with its sculptural, tactile qualities, its deeply rooted symbolism and simply for the look of it and the way it catches the light.

Metal thread work is such an intriguing part of embroidery for many reasons, but perhaps part of its allure is the glamour that it evokes with all its embedded associations in our psyche and across so many differing cultural, political and religious backgrounds.

Let us not forget the qualities of the metal itself, which has an innate warmth and universal appeal. It is no surprise that almost every civilisation has revered this metal and used it to celebrate the most important landmarks in their lives. Some might say that this is the chosen material of the elite, used to emphasise their elevated status.

It is tactile before even being worked, becomes more so through the craftsmanship and diligence of our splendid gold and silver wyre drawers, and is enhanced by the artisan hand embroiderers who strive to use this most popular of techniques to better what has gone before and bring beauty to others through their efforts.

The subtle manipulation of the padding, type and size of metal thread chosen, the direction in which the thread is stitched, and the colour chosen to hold the metal thread down, create a delicate shift in the way the textile reflects the light and can alter it from simply being a flat embroidery to a piece which interacts with the light. The light – and therefore the viewer's eye – should dance across its surface.

A particularly intriguing facet to the art of metal-thread embroidery is the fact that it is an ever-changing art form, not only in style of design but also in its basest form; the very thread with which you work is made to change. The tarnishing process is a natural part of this technique to the extent that some might call goldwork the study of elegant decay. It is this response to time, damp, heat and the air – all of the elements, in truth, that we ourselves respond to – which ultimately makes metal thread work fascinating to me. It emphasises the limits to my control. I may be able to spend hours fashioning the thread into a beautiful embroidery but ultimately it will be fashioned by greater forces than myself. And everybody reacts to that fact differently: some try to control this alteration, with airtight frames, carefully controlled room temperature and storage conditions, or simply by their choice of threads. Others embrace the unpredictability of the alterations. It is truly a technique which encourages you to embrace the differences not only in it but also in yourself!

I hope that this essential stitch guide helps to introduce you to a subject which offers so much variety and encourages you to try a new technique, and also that it will offer a sound reminder of the traditional methods of metal-thread hand embroidery for those of you who have used this technique before but need a helping hand to iron out any general problems. There is, of course, a limit to what can be achieved in a book of this size when handling a subject which is so varied, but when used in combination, the given techniques will keep you endlessly occupied in hours of happy, sometimes challenging but hopefully always productive stitching.

Above: section of an altar frontal featuring high-relief goldwork over card padding with chain stitch or tambour work in silk on a cream silk satin ground. (RSN Collection)

THE HISTORY OF METAL THREAD WORK

As suggested earlier, goldwork has become synonymous with splendour and as such was utilised in many countries by various cultures and faiths. What can be seen as a common thread between all of them is that the ability to have finely rendered and embellished goods, particularly those made in gold, has always been used as an indicator of wealth, power and status. As such, the history of goldwork really deserves an in-depth study, however, if we look at some of the important development features in relation to the Royal School of Needlework, it may be easier to tackle this subject.

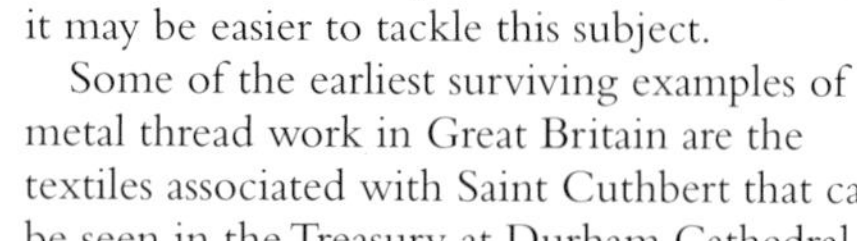

Some of the earliest surviving examples of metal thread work in Great Britain are the textiles associated with Saint Cuthbert that can be seen in the Treasury at Durham Cathedral. These are vestments in the form of a stole and maniple and date to the tenth century. It is interesting to note that on these early pieces of church textiles, golden threads acted as a decorative surround or background to throw the fine embroidered detail into the fore. This use of gold as a dazzling background became honed during the medieval period in England, a period in which this work became known as Opus Anglicanum (English work). It was the skilful rendering of goldwork in a technique called underside couching at this time that helped to make this work so famous and highly sought after. It was, in fact, so highly prized that it was used as political gifts across Europe.

One of the reasons that the Church used gold was to celebrate the majesty of God. May Morris, who taught at the RSN during the Victorian period, noted: 'The old workers knew what they were about when they lavished mysterious splendour of gold and broken colour on their altar apparel and priests' vestments; such a method lost little through distance of its power of impressing the spectator with a vague sense of beauty and richness entirely appropriate to the spirit of the building'.

Left: silk crane on goldwork ground. Japanese, twentieth-century, Jean Panter bequest. (RSN Collection 1474)

Right: peacocks in heavy metal thread work with silk. Indian, nineteenth or twentieth century. (RSN Collection T33)

Nineteenth-century envelope case from India, which contained greetings to Queen Victoria. Metal thread embroidery on red velvet. (RSN Collection)

Later, gold was used in secular embroidery, which was seen as a reflection of the divine right of kings, although there is far less of this early secular embroidery still in existence. This may be due to the huge costs involved in the materials alone. These valuable metal threads were often recycled or even melted down, a technique known as drizzling and parfilage.

It is important to remember that during this early period there was a strict hierarchy in place, but equally this meant that a churchman and a king had appearances to uphold – after all, they had been favoured by God for high placement. During a time of widespread illiteracy, the impact of the written word was restricted but this gave images and the visual realm more power over the senses and the mind. These images would be used to inform and mould your audience. The pomp and circumstance created by the awe-inspiring use of metal threads in church work was observed keenly by kings and emulated where possible. We still see evidence of this today in the use of golden braids and embroidery in military uniforms, court dress and ceremonial items such as the imposing Lord Chancellor's purse, the most recent of which was worked by the RSN with mixed techniques (including many that can be seen in this stitch guide) over high-relief padding, lending a sculptural effect to the impressive finished piece.

Close-up of a sampler featuring counted patterns in silk and metal threads. English, late eighteenth century. (RSN Collection 215)

There are also, of course, the Robes of Estate of our monarchs. The RSN has been honoured to design and produce the embroidery for both Queen Elizabeth the Queen Mother and for our current Queen Elizabeth. This is a wonderful opportunity for us to honour our patrons and play a small, if vital, part in the spectacle of the Coronation Day. The embroidery is used only on the female robes, the male robes having only golden braid. The chosen symbols for the Coronation robe are extremely significant as they are meant to represent what that monarch hopes for in her reign to come. The Queen Mother, for example, chose flora and fauna from some of the Commonwealth countries to show that her interests lay in the Commonwealth as a whole, whereas the Queen chose wheat sheaves and barley ears to represent peace and prosperity, which is what the Queen and in fact the whole country hoped for in the post World War Two period.

The embroidery on the robes is a mixture of standard and complex metal thread techniques worked to the highest traditional technical level. Multiple embroiderers work on the robes at the same time and each had to stitch in a uniform way to give the impression that only one hand had embroidered them. This, in itself, can be a complex process, but add to that the time constraints and you can appreciate that the Robes of Estate are a unique chance to showcase the extraordinary craftsmanship, attention to detail and loyal discretion with which the RSN is synonymous.

This technique requires discipline, understanding, patience and careful handling alongside creativity, attention to detail and the desire to mix tactile sculpting with striving to achieve the elusive beautiful light play across the surface that has been created. It is a combination of all of these factors which has led to the longevity of our love affair with metal thread work, a love affair which continues today and thankfully shows no signs of abating. It seems that we are still held enthralled by the splendour of gold both on a primitive instinctual level and from a purely aesthetic perspective.

Ante-pendium (altar hanging), designed by Matthew Webb and worked by the RSN in silk and metal threads. English, twentieth century. (RSN Collection 101)

MATERIALS AND EQUIPMENT

There are certain materials and pieces of equipment that are essential when it comes to creating a piece of metal thread work. It is important to choose a ground fabric which is substantial enough to support the threads. If this is not the case then you will need to add a layer of calico underneath to provide the strength required for this technique. It is important to work on taut fabric and this can be achieved by using a frame. There are also tools which will aid your embroidery, all of which are explained in the sections below.

FRAMES

It is always easier to stitch and maintain stitch tension when the fabric itself is under good tension, and the best way to do this is to use a frame. There are a number of different types of frame and the first thing that you will need to do is decide which is most appropriate for the project you have in mind.

The first option is a ring frame, which should be used for small, short-term projects. Both rings in the frame should be bound with thin cotton, calico or bias binding before use and this will help to keep the embroidery fabric clean and taut. To help to tighten the frame once the fabric is in it, use a screwdriver and then use both hands to ease the fabric until it is drum tight. As you embroider, the fabric will loosen and you will need to use both hands to pull it tight again.

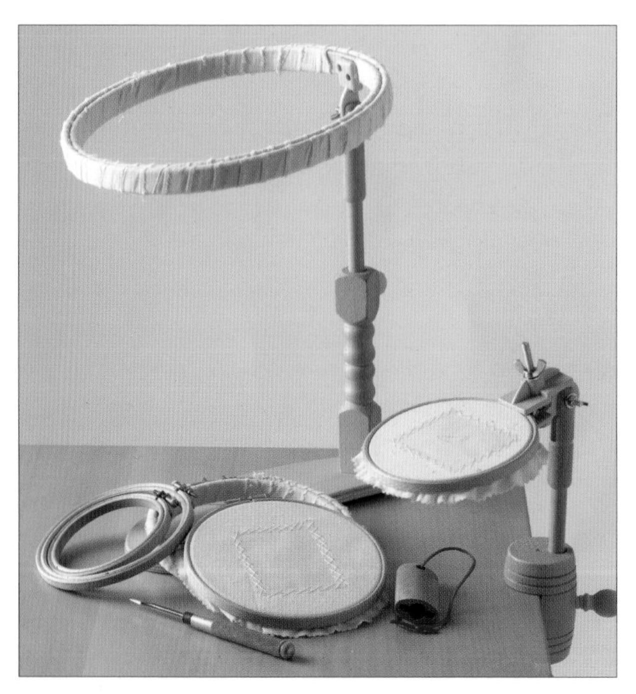

A selection of ring frames, including a seat frame (at the back), a barrel clamp and hand-held varieties (some wrapped in calico). Also shown are a screwdriver and wingnut clamp to assist in frame tightening.

A slate frame and trestles.

It is important to maintain the clean, fresh appearance of your embroidery and fabric, and covering your work with white acid-free tissue paper and exposing only the working area will help you to do this. The working area should then be covered with tissue paper when you are not working on it. Whilst this is good practice for short periods of time away from your embroidery, for longer periods of time the fabric should be removed from the ring frame so that a round mark or bruise does not mar the fabric.

Although you can purchase hand-held ring frames, at the RSN we tend to prefer ones which attach to a barrel clamp to be supported by a table, a seat frame or floor stand. All of these latter options enable you to work with both hands, which should give you more control, speed and comfort when stitching.

Roller frames or, preferably, slate frames tend to be more appropriate for larger or longer-term projects. For instructions on how to frame up a slate, roller or ring frame, please refer to the appropriate section (see pages 24–29). A slate frame will also keep your working fabric under good tension and allow you to work with both hands, which should give you more control, speed and comfort when stitching in the same way that the ring frame does. Slate frames are rested on top of trestles, which are comfortable to sit at, can be adjusted to complement your height, and can even be angled slightly if that is what you prefer.

METAL THREADS

I always liked the look of metal thread embroidery, but before it was explained to me, the subject seemed unfeasibly complicated! The thing to note, however, is that it is very much like any other form of embroidery in so far as it has a variety of different threads, all of which have their own names and most of which are available in a variety of sizes. They also have specific purposes. Once you become familiar with the differences between these threads and learn how to handle them, there is an almost infinite variety of ways in which they can be used.

There are numerous types of metal threads that can be purchased, but as a guide they can be divided into the following categories:

Gold-plated metal tends never to have more than two per cent gold content.

Gilt-plated metal tends to have approximately 0.5 per cent gold content.

Silver metal contains a maximum of ninety nine per cent fine silver.

Silver-plated metal has a silver content of no more than 1.5 per cent.

Copper metal tends to be either hard drawn or to consist of copper alloys.

The following section should help you to identify the various threads a little easier and become more confident with your thread handling.

Spring Flight *(detail)*

Helen McCook

Worked in assorted silver, golden, copper and bronze metal threads; spangles; and a variety of colours of stranded cotton threads to silk dupion ground.

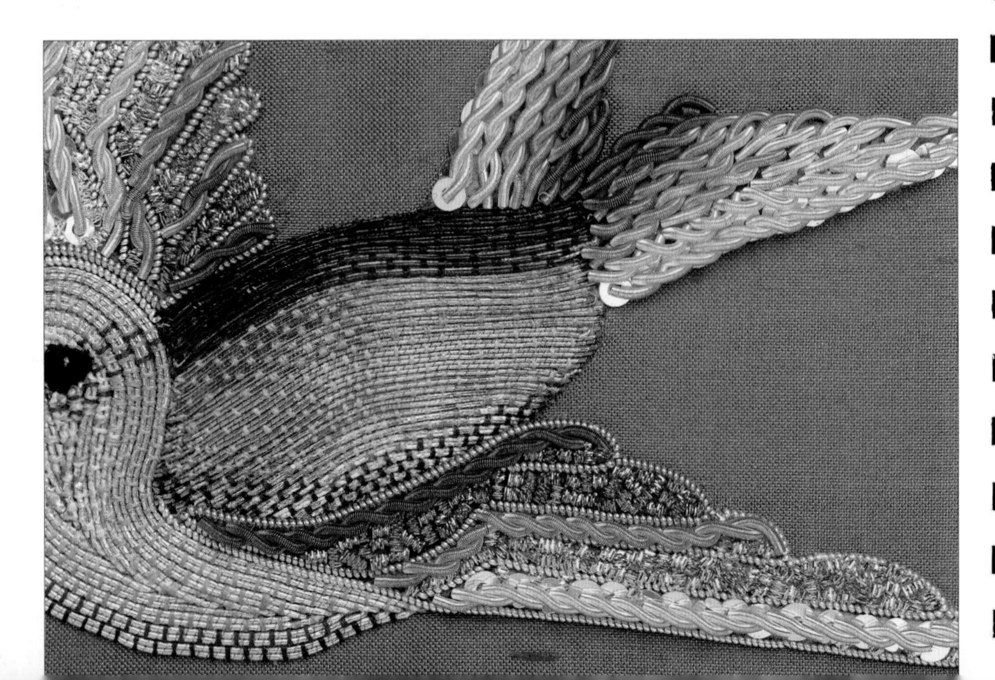

Couching threads

These are threads that are applied to the surface of the fabric, generally in pairs, and are held down with a small holding stitch (see couching section on pages 45–51). They tend to have ends that can unravel or fray and therefore the ends of the threads are later plunged through the surface of the fabric to the back of the embroidery and fastened with additional overstitches. Any excess thread is then neatly snipped off.

Threads that come into this category include the following:

Japanese gold is essentially composed of a thread core with flat, paper-backed gold wrapped around it.

Passing has a thread core which is twisted in one direction, and the fine metal thread is then wrapped neatly over the core in the opposite direction, resulting in a reasonably strong and stable thread. Wavy passing has a rougher finish and is far rarer than the more commonly used smooth passing.

Twist is generally composed of three metal-wrapped cores which are then twisted around each other to produce something very similar to a cord.

Elizabethan twist is a much finer version of the twist mentioned above and, instead of being three-ply, is generally two-ply. It is slightly different from the other threads in this category in so far as it can be used in a needle to sew through the fabric as well as being couched with.

Rococco is composed of a central, twisted-thread core which is then wrapped with another thread to create a wavy effect. The whole core is then neatly wrapped with a fine metal thread in the opposite direction to the twist. Rococco threads have a gentle open-wave effect.

Check is made in much the same way as rococco thread, but has a tighter effect with its waved pattern.

Pearl purl is made with wires that are considerably thicker than the wires used to make the other purl threads (see page 18). It is therefore far more robust, in many senses, than the others. The wire is beaded into a horseshoe or stirrup shape and then wrapped around itself into a coil.

A variety of metal couching threads on reels (check, passing, twist and Japanese).

Cutwork threads (purls)

There are a number of different purl threads, but they all have certain characteristics in common: they are made of a wire which is tightly coiled like a spring; they do not fray and therefore do not need to have their ends taken through to the back of the fabric to be fastened off; and they should be stitched invisibly so that you do not see the stitch attaching them to the face of the fabric. These threads should be handled carefully so that they are not damaged or overstretched and therefore rendered useless for traditional goldwork embroidery effects. If this happens, you should store them separately for possible use on creative metal thread projects at a later date.

Spangles, seed beads, whipped plate, kid, pearl purl, smooth and bright check threads in copper, gold and silver metals.

Threads that come into this category include the following:

Smooth purl is essentially a round, spring-like thread but the surface of its metal has been burnished or flattened slightly so that it is very shiny.

Rough purl is made the same way as smooth purl but the surface of the metal is left rounded and therefore has a more matt appearance than the smooth purl.

Bright check is made in a similar way to smooth purl and is also shiny, but instead of being spring-like and circular in appearance, the coils have angles added at regular intervals that catch the light.

Wire or **dull check** is made in the same way as bright check but is matt in appearance in a similar way to rough purl.

MISCELLANEOUS MATERIALS

There are, of course, any number of materials which can be combined with metal thread embroidery to create interesting effects, for example washers, screws, safety pins and jewellery findings, but for a traditional approach we are left with items such as kid leather, spangles and plate. There are sections dedicated to the basic application of each of these techniques further on in the book.

Kid leather is a supple leather which has been treated to have a metallic finish on one side. Alternatives to animal hide can be purchased according to the financial or ethical leanings of the individual. It should be noted that some metalised faux kid can lose its flexibility and develop the appearance of cracks as it dries out over time.

Spangles are essentially metal sequins, however they all have a small slit to one side due to the manufacturing process. Spangles are made of tightly coiled, heavy wire which is cut and flattened. Each cut coil produces one spangle, the cut being evident in the spangles still as the aforementioned slit.

Plate or **broad plate**, to give it its traditional name, consists of a piece of wire which has been flattened by rollers enough times to achieve the sufficiently smooth width. Other members of the plate family are whipped plate, which has a fine thread wrapped around the plate to create an alternative effect, and crinkle plate, which sees an even ribble or crinkle put into the metal with shaped rollers.

There are, of course, many other threads and braids but these are the ones which are used most often and therefore the most useful to mention in a beginner's stitch guide.

FABRICS

Metal thread work is traditionally worked on rich fabrics to complement the richness of the thread, the most commonly used fabrics being jewel-coloured silks and velvets. However, this technique can essentially be worked on any fabric. On the whole, the fabric is applied to a calico base to help strengthen and support the fabric and metal thread work. To see how to do this, refer to the section in the book on 'framing up' (pages 24–29).

An assortment of fabrics including velvet, silk dupion, satin and organza.

EMBROIDERY THREADS

There are no hard-and-fast rules regarding which embroidery threads you should use in combination with metal threads. It is very much a case of personal preference and choice of colour palette to complement your design. For most goldwork designs you will require self-coloured thread (a thread to match the colour of the metal) and contrasting shades to create impact.

A variety of embroidery threads including silk, stranded cottons and machine threads.

SEWING TOOLS

A good tool box for an embroiderer should include sharp dressmakers' shears, sharp embroidery scissors, needles and curved needles, sewing threads, paper scissors, fine dressmakers' pins (preferably stored in a pincushion or needlecase for ease of use), a tape measure, a small screwdriver (for use with ring frames to tighten the screw), pointed tweezers, a stiletto (in case you need to make small holes for decoration or to aid with plunging ends if there are many layers of padding), a small pair of pliers (to pull the needle through the fabric if there are a lot of layers), parcel string and a bracing needle (for framing up on a slate frame).

Scissors and sheaths, which help to maintain your scissors' blades and tips in good condition whilst they are not in use.

Needles

The needles most commonly used are sizes 9, 10 and 12 embroidery needles as they pass comfortably through the gold for cutwork. You need to remember that the smaller the size of the gold, the finer the needle will need to be to pass through the purl. A larger needle may be utilised for use with a lasso to plunge ends (generally a size 18 chenille needle or a size 18 tapestry needle). Curved needles can be very useful when tying threads off on the back of the embroidery (though some people prefer a straight embroidery needle).

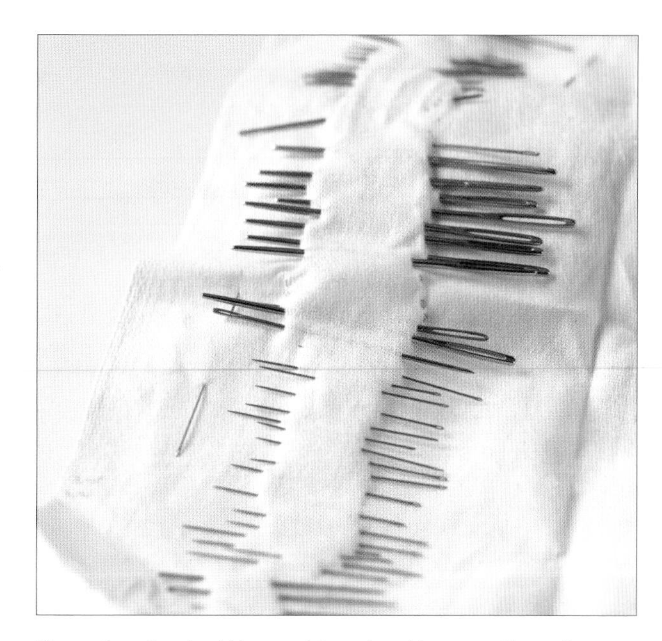

Pins and needles should be stored in a pincushion or needlecase for ease of use.

Other sewing tools

Other tools which are especially useful to the embroiderer wishing to work with metal threads are as follows:

White acid-free tissue paper is important to keep your embroidery project clean. Use it to cover the surface of the fabric where you are not currently working.

Wax: there are many types of wax and wax-related products available, however the one which consistently yields the best results is pure beeswax. This is used to coat the working thread (usually a Gutermann sewing thread) to smooth and strengthen it, which will ease the use of the metal threads and help to prevent any sharp ends from catching and stretching.

A mellor is a metal tool with one wide rounded end and one tapered pointed end. The rounded end is used to help mould the shape of couched or cut metal threads and the pointed end can be used to help manipulate the threads with more precision. The tapered blade is used to manipulate cut threads over so that they bend easier, thus reducing the likelihood of any cracks and blemishes occurring.

Tweezers can be used for manipulating the metal threads and helping to withdraw threads if any problems have occurred while stitching. They can also be very helpful when using pearl purl to aid in the working of sharp points or when trying to merge two ends together to close a shape, for example a circle.

Gold scissors look like normal embroidery scissors but have a very sharp point and the blades are serrated to help cut the gold without crushing it and without it rolling out of the blades.

An assortment of useful tools: a gold board, mellor, thimbles, pins, needles, curved needles, a bracing needle, a mechanical pencil, a fine paintbrush, a pricker, tweezers, a waterproof fine-line marker pen, watercolour and gouache paint, beeswax, a tape measure and a paint palette.

Thimbles: not everybody feels comfortable using thimbles, however there are a number of different types which you can purchase including rubber, metal and leather, and there is bound to be one that you are happy using. To aid your feeling of comfort with a thimble, make sure you get one that actually fits your finger. Thimbles are worn on the middle finger on both hands and will prove very useful when pushing your needle through multiple layers of padding.

Gold board: this is board which has velvet on both sides. The velvet on the lower side ensures that the board may rest on areas which have already been embroidered and the velvet on the upper surface is used to nestle the gold against that will be cut (for cutwork, see pages 58–64). The pile of the velvet helps to keep the gold still while you are measuring it and also stops any cut pieces from rolling around and escaping before they can be stitched down.

Webbing, calico, felt and string

Webbing is used during framing up (see pages 24–29) and calico makes a good, firm backing fabric to support metal thread work. There are various methods of padding associated with goldwork, for which felt and string are required. Traditionally, yellow craft felt and carpet felt are used, and soft and hard string, depending on the method used (see pages 38-43).

Webbing for use during framing up; calico to use as a backing fabric; craft felt for craft-felt padding; soft string and hard string for soft- and hard-string padding respectively.

Equipment for transferring a design

There are a number of ways to transfer a design (see pages 32-33), but the most common method is prick and pounce, for which you will need a pricker. Paints are used to mark the design on the fabric, generally either watercolour or gouache as these can be mixed finely and are quite easy to remove. Oil paints tend to be used on items for outdoor use as they do not tend to run if they become moist. You will also need a paint palette to mix an appropriate colour and a fine paintbrush. If you decide to use a light box, it may be more appropriate to use a fine pen to mark the design on to the fabric.

Framing up

It is very important to frame up your fabric so that it is taut and stretched evenly. This will help you to achieve an even finish and make it easier to maintain a good tension in your embroidery. Fabric in a frame is easier to protect than unframed fabric as it may be covered and stored without any creases or folds appearing. The fabric tension sometimes eases off during periods of intense work and so it is important to remember to re-tighten the frame regularly by adjusting the string at the sides. Once the frame is tight it should be rested on a pair of trestles which should be height adjusted to create a comfortable working position for you to sit at.

PREPARING A SLATE FRAME

Slate frames are made up of four wooden lengths – two rollers with webbing attached and two stretchers with holes for pegs or split pins. This is the best type of frame for larger projects, as it allows you to get your fabric as taut as possible.

On first use, it is advisable to mark the centre of each of the rollers to ensure that you attach your fabric squarely.

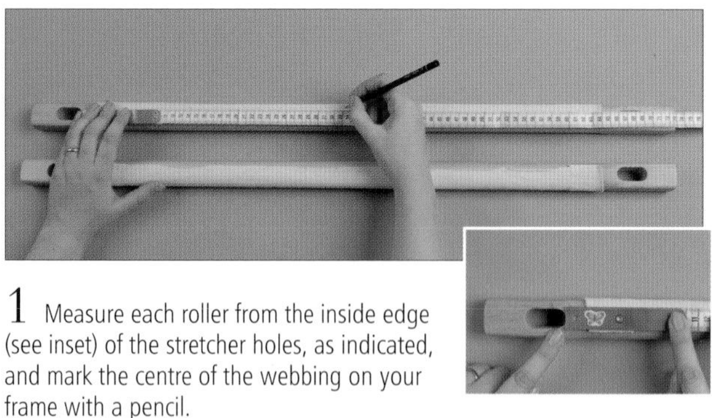

1 Measure each roller from the inside edge (see inset) of the stretcher holes, as indicated, and mark the centre of the webbing on your frame with a pencil.

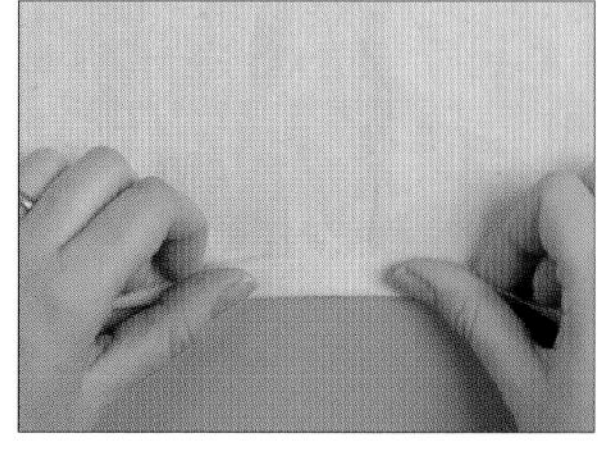

2 The top and bottom of the backing fabric should be attached to the rollers first. Fold the bottom edge of the calico along the grain of the fabric 1.5cm (½in) under itself as shown. Repeat on the top edge.

3 Fold the backing fabric in half, bringing the folded corners to meet each other at the bottom. Push a pin through the crease to mark the centre.

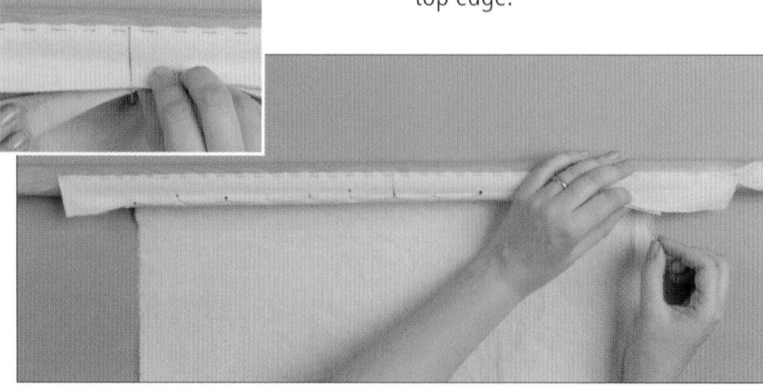

4 Align the centre of the folded edge with the point marked on the webbing (see inset). Pinning from the centre point outwards, pin the folded edge to the back of the webbing, sandwiching the 1.5cm (½in) length between the webbing and the back of the calico.

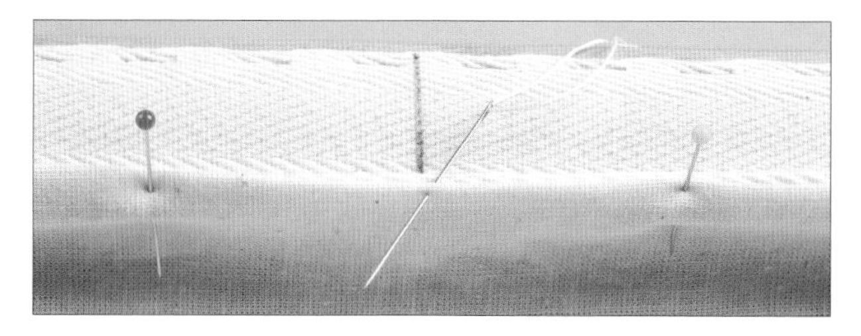

5 Thread a size 5 crewel needle with buttonhole thread and tie a knot in the end. Starting at the central point of the fabric, remove the pin and take your needle through the webbing to the front, hiding the knot between the webbing and the calico.

6 Stitch the calico to the webbing by oversewing them. Work out from the centre to ensure that the calico is secured smoothly and evenly, removing the pins as you work. Once you reach the end of the calico oversew a few extra stitches to secure; then work outwards to the other side from the centre in the same way. Repeat the process on the other roller.

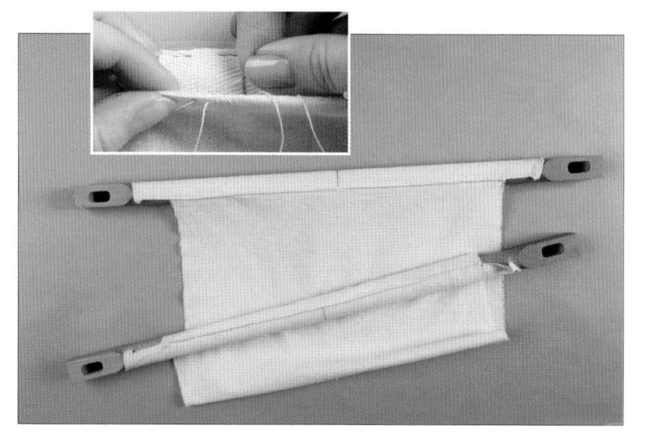

Note

Decide how far to roll in the rollers before inserting the two stretcher bars. This can enable you to sit closer to your work when stitching, which may make your working more comfortable.

7 Insert the stretchers into each side of the rollers, making sure they line up with each other. Insert pegs or split pins into the holes to hold the rollers away from each other. Keep the fabric taut and gradually increase the distance between the pegs on alternate stretchers.

Note

The holes on the stretcher bars are a mirror image of each other, so you can use them to ensure an even tension.

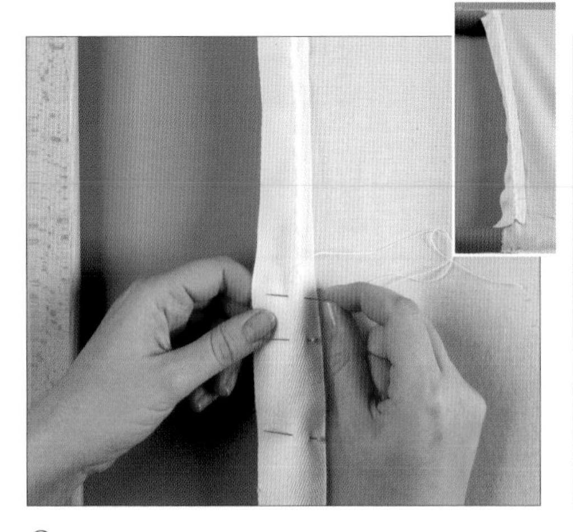

8 Measure the distance between the rollers and cut a length of cotton webbing tape to the same length. Place it on the side edge of the calico, and pin it into position, three quarters over the linen and one quarter off the linen. Fasten it to the calico with buttonhole thread with horizontal stitches as shown (see inset).

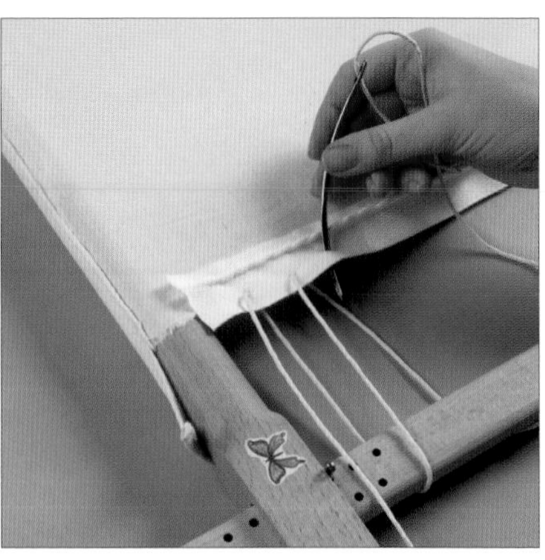

9 Thread your bracing needle with a ball of string and place the ball on the floor. Take the sharp end of the bracing needle down through the overhanging area of the cotton webbing tape and pull through a good length of string. Take the bracing needle underneath and up around the stretcher and back through the cotton tape every 2.5cm (1in).

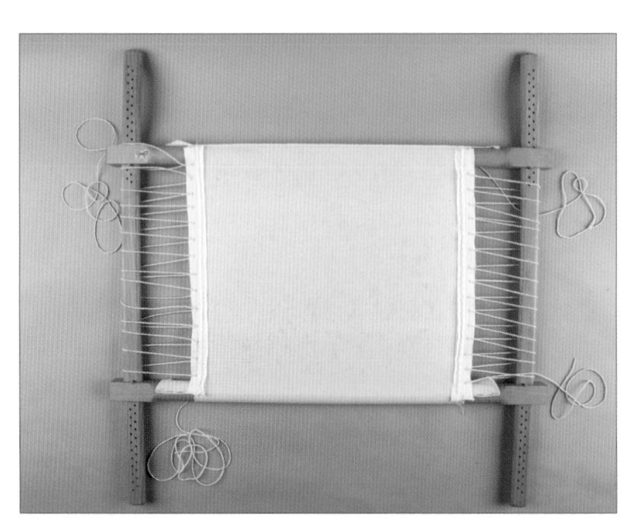

10 Leave a good length of string at each end before cutting and repeat on the other side.

11 Cut a piece of fabric to the size you wish to work, and secure it in place in the centre of the backing fabric, with a pin in each side and in each corner as shown.

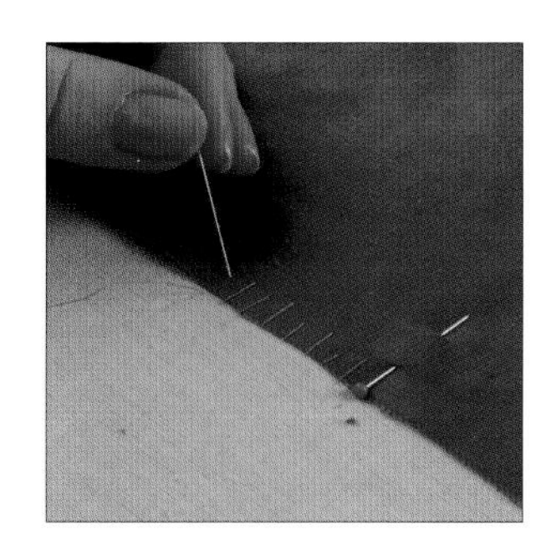

12 Thread a size 9 or 10 embroidery needle with strong sewing thread. Starting from the centre of one of the sides, work alternate long and short stitches as shown, up to the corner.

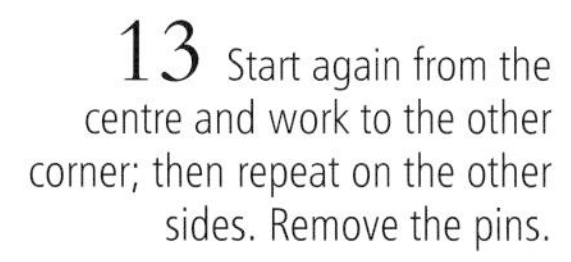

13 Start again from the centre and work to the other corner; then repeat on the other sides. Remove the pins.

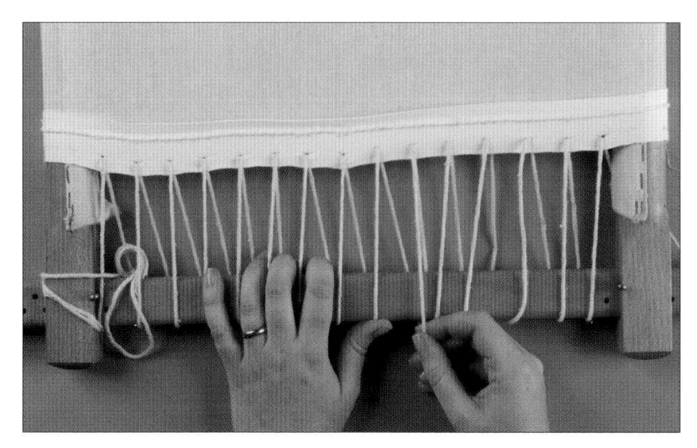

14 Starting from the centre of each of the attached cotton tape strings, pull each loop taut and hold it. Work to the side and secure the string with a slip knot before working back to the other side. Work gradually to avoid pulling the fabric off-centre, retightening the knots gradually until the calico and top fabric feels firm.

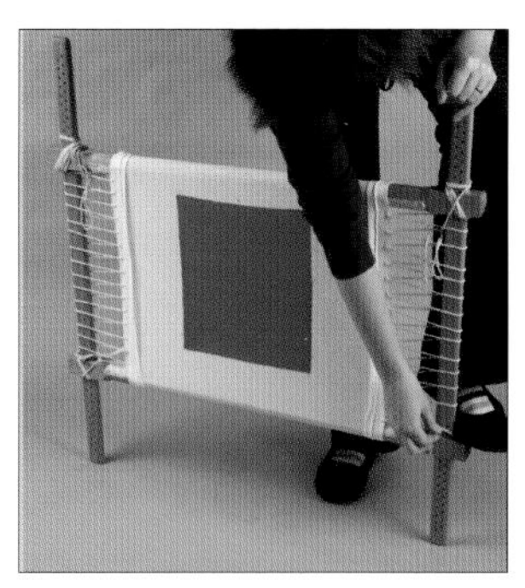

15 Stand the base of the frame upright on the floor and use the sole of your foot to push down each end of the bottom roller. Move the pegs individually, and one hole at a time, to increase the distance between the pegs and tighten the fabric.

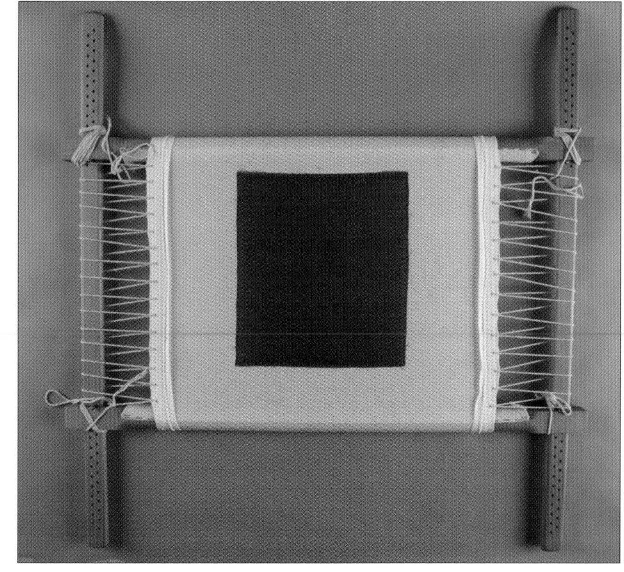

16 Repeat step 15 until the fabric is drum tight, and secure the strings to finish.

PREPARING ROLLER FRAMES

This type of frame is a smaller version of a slate frame. Roller frames will not keep your fabric quite as taut as a slate frame, but they are portable and more readily available.

1 Follow steps 1–10 on pages 24–26 for preparing a slate frame, inserting the ends of the rollers into the ends of the stretcher at step 7. Turn the frame over.

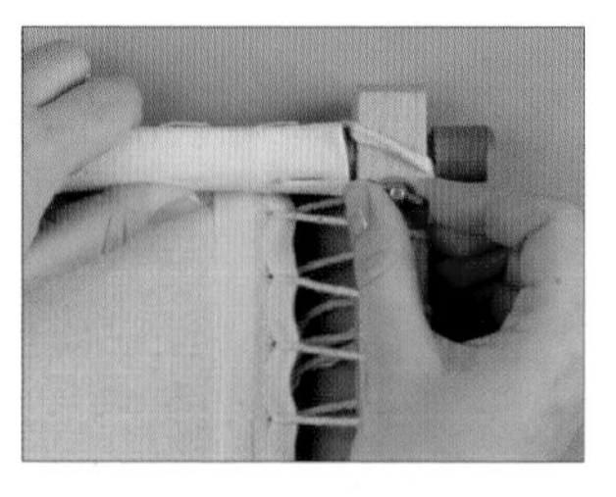

2 Roll the bar up to tighten the fabric, then tighten the wingnuts to secure.

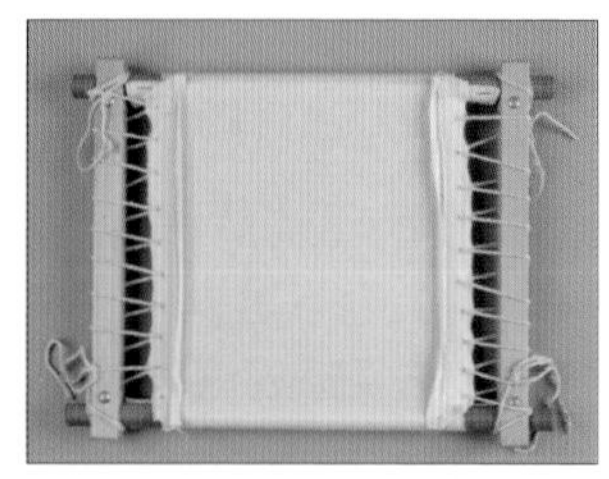

A prepared roller frame.

PREPARING INTERLOCKING BAR FRAMES

Interlocking bar frames are known as stretcher bars in the US, and are great for small projects. You can make the frames exactly the size you want and they are quick to frame up. They are also good value for money and readily available.

1 Assemble the bars into the size of frame that you want for your project. Place your fabric on top.

2 Press a drawing pin into the centre of one side then, keeping the fabric taut, add one opposite. Repeat on the other sides to secure the fabric to the frame.

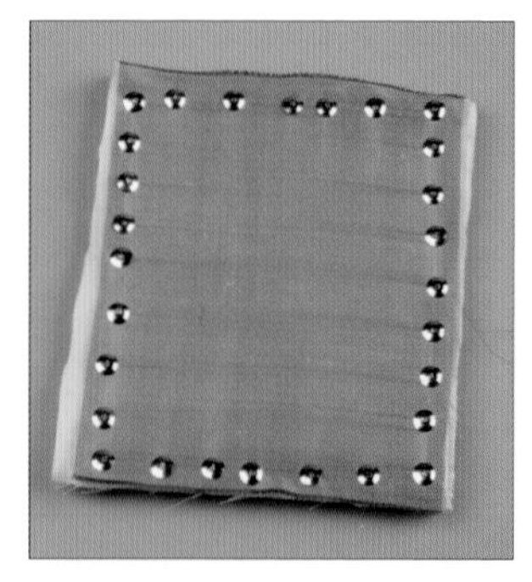

3 Secure the embroidery fabric completely by pinning the corners, then adding additional pins along the sides.

PREPARING A RING FRAME

Ring frames come in lots of sizes and are readily available, easy to frame up and portable. However, they do not keep the fabric very tight and so are best used for small projects.

1 Wrap bias binding around both rings individually, being careful to overlap the binding as you work. When you reach the end, trim the excess and secure it in place with a stitch. This will make the frame tighter, maintain fabric tension and reduce potential damage to the fabric.

2 Put the inner ring inside the outer ring and tighten the outer ring by twisting the screw until it is finger tight.

3 Remove the inner ring, then place the outer ring flat on the table. Place the fabric and backing fabric over the ring.

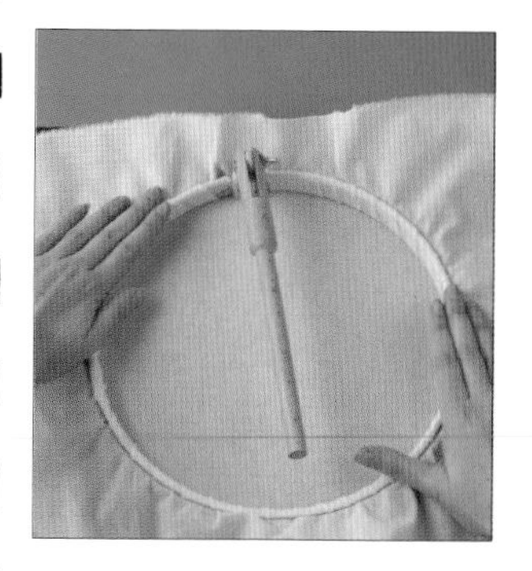

4 Lay the fabric flat, then press the inner ring into position, trapping the fabric layers.

5 Turn the frame over and use a screwdriver to tighten the frame.

A prepared ring frame.

DESIGN

Virtually any design can be adapted for use and interpretation with metal thread work, as the range of threads and varied ways of working and applying the threads offer huge versatility and endless possibilities.

One of the most important aspects of metal thread work design is texture. Our talented gold and silver wyre drawers go to great lengths to cunningly create a sparkling array of threads made in a variety of ways to enable us, as embroiderers, to have as many options as possible when it comes to stitching using this technique. Arguably the major reason for the importance of texture is that light bounces off different textures in various ways, and it is the play of light across a piece of metal thread work, in conjunction with its combinations of textures, that can really make it interesting, or otherwise. Therefore it is important to look at combining different textures to get different effects. You should also look at ways of enhancing the qualities of different gold threads, for example certain types of threads may suit different areas of your design. You can also sometimes be limited to what type of thread goes where.

Just as we appreciate light by understanding the depth of darkness, so too we should appreciate that no piece of embroidery should be a solid mass of stitch. There should be a harmonious blend of boldly and heavily worked areas foiled against a backdrop of delicacy and lightly worked open spaces. It takes both to make us truly appreciate the differences they offer.

Think carefully about the flow of the lines within the piece. This can be altered drastically depending on the direction in which you lay your metal couching threads or the angle in which you stitch down your cutwork, for example. I find drawing the different options for the flow of gold on to a photocopy of the outline design particularly helpful when pondering this issue.

Outline diagram.

Shading plan.

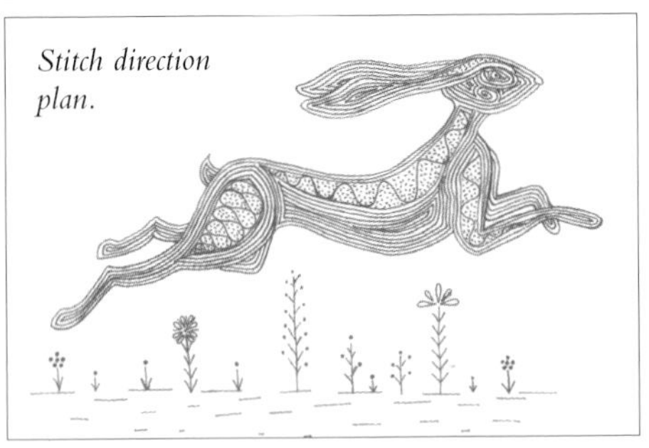
Stitch direction plan.

Colour plan.

The stages in the development of my design for 'Fearless Freedom'. I may also draw up a stitch plan, in which I write my initial stitch choices on to the stitch direction plan.

Once you have thought about and learnt the rules above, you can apply them to any design. Having done so, you should think about the height of your padding across the piece. Metal thread embroidery works in the realm of three dimensions and you should utilise all of the padding techniques appropriate to your chosen design to enhance your work further.

You could additionally consider introducing coloured threads into your metal thread work and experiment with shade play across the piece. This could be abstract, pattern based or to aid the three-dimensional effect. Again, I find it helpful to draw on to a copy of the outline design to aid me with this. There is, however, no right or wrong way of approaching this and as you become more experienced in working with metal threads, you will be able to trust more to instinct and less to rigid planning.

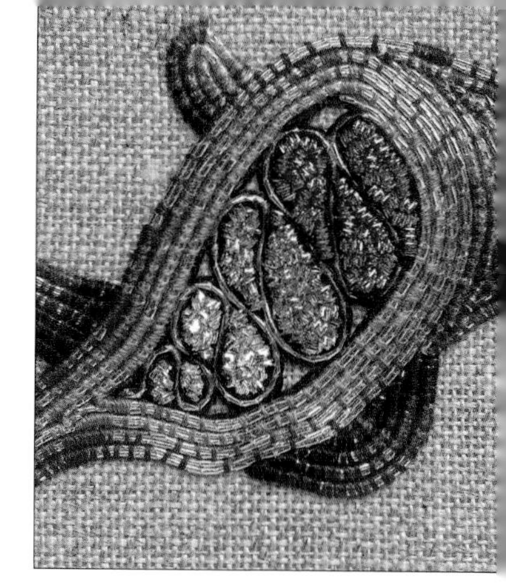

Enlarged view of the stitching on the hare's leg.

Fearless Freedom

Helen McCook

The finished piece. Japanese thread, copper, gilt and silver bright check thread, and assorted stranded cotton threads to linen ground.

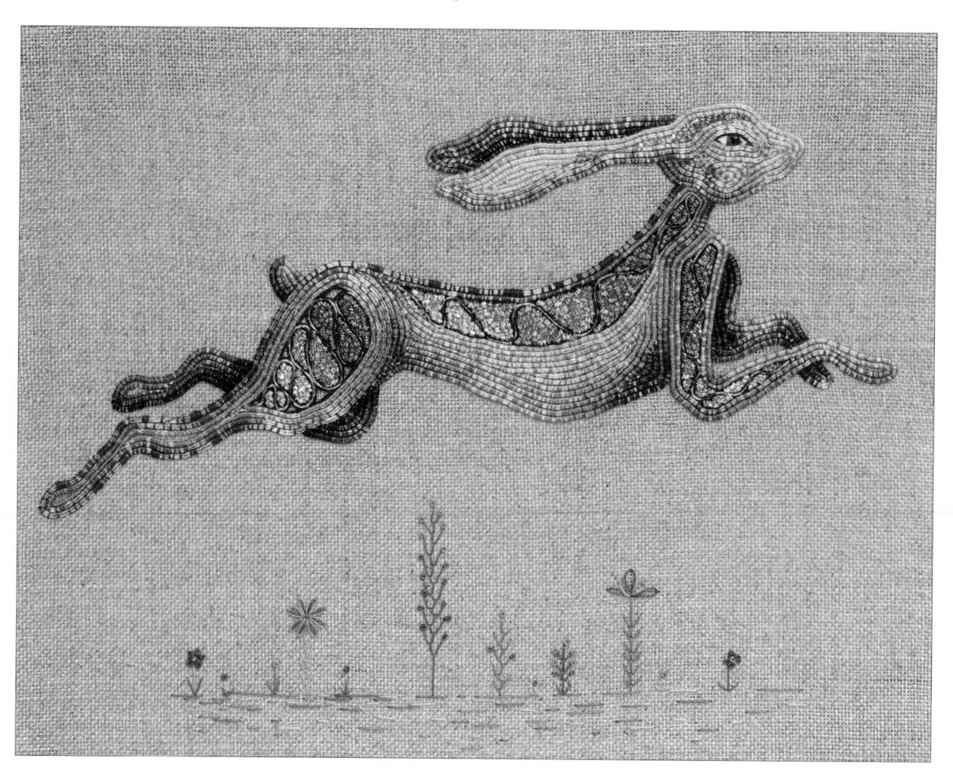

TRANSFERRING THE DESIGN

There are several ways to transfer your design on to fabric but the most commonly used technique is the traditional prick-and-pounce method.

Prick-and-pounce method

First, finalise your design and draw its outlines on to tracing paper. Now place a small, sharp needle into a pricker (a small vice) and place the tracing paper over a wad of fabric, backing or a soft cushion. Make small pin holes with the point of the needle in the pricker at regular intervals across the outline of the whole design, approximately 2mm ($^1/_{16}$in) apart. Hold the tracing paper up to the light so that you can check that you have pricked all of the lines that are needed.

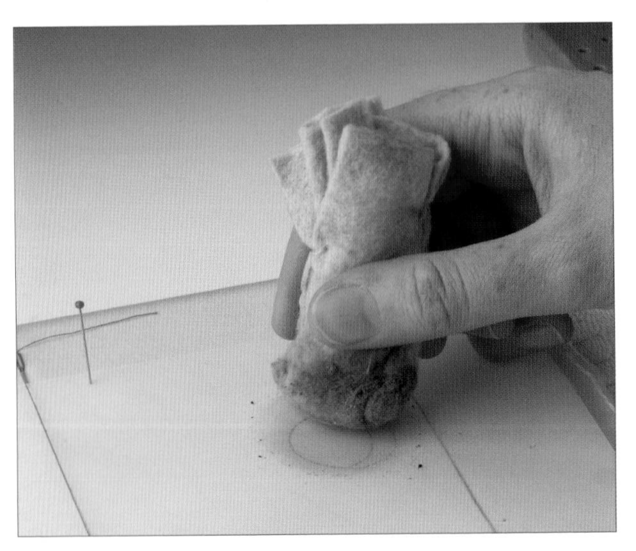

Next, pin your tracing paper on to the chosen fabric for your embroidery (this should be framed up and taut). Take a fabric roll and dip it into the pounce and rub in slow, smooth circles across the surface of your design until you feel confident that you have covered the whole piece. You may then gently lift up one corner of the tracing paper to make certain that the pounce has dropped through the pricked holes. The next step is to lift off the tracing paper and pour any excess pounce back into its pot to be re-used.

Now you need to mix some yellow ochre gouache paint with a little white gouache and water until you have a golden-coloured paint which has the consistency of single cream. Take an extremely fine paintbrush and carefully paint over the design lines, which are currently shown in pounce. Once you have finished all of the painting and it has had time to dry, turn your frame over and gently beat the back of your fabric with the back of a baby brush to dislodge any excess pounce. Flip you frame back over to the front and use the baby brush's soft bristles to careful brush off any remaining traces of pounce. Cover all fabric with white acid-free tissue paper, except for the small area that you will work on first.

Note

You can make your own pounce using a pestle and mortar or you can purchase it already made. White pounce is made of crushed-up, dried cuttlefish bones. Black pounce is made of crushed-up charcoal and grey is a mixture of the two. Black is used on mid-coloured fabrics, white is used on dark-coloured fabrics and grey is used on light-coloured fabrics.

Light-box method

A quick alternative to the prick-and-pounce method, if you are working a small project and using a smooth fabric such as silk, is to use a quilting pencil or waterproof fine-line artist's pen and a light box.

STARTING TO STITCH

THREADING A NEEDLE

To thread the needle, make sure that the thread is small enough to fit through the eye of the chosen needle and that the needle is appropriate to the chosen embroidery technique, fabric and thread. Cut the end of the thread so that it is not frayed and then press the very end of the thread between the cushiony parts of your fingertips so that only a tiny dot of the thread is visible. Take the eye to the dot of thread and, in theory, there is nowhere for the thread to go but through the eye of the needle.

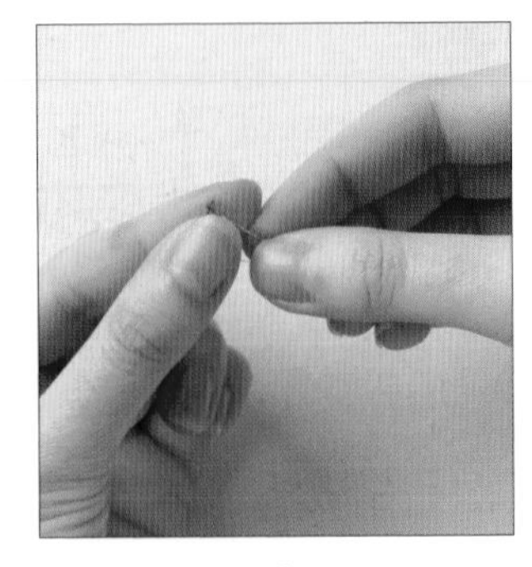

Threading a needle.

STARTING A THREAD

At the RSN we tend to use a technique known as the waste-knot technique to start and finish the working thread. To begin, first thread up a needle, tie a knot in the other end of your thread and then find the area where you wish to start stitching.

> *Note*
>
> *It is not cheating to use a needle threader if you find it helpful!*

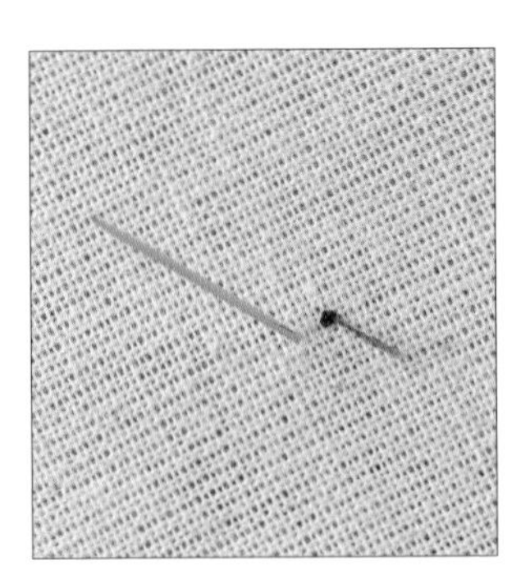

1 Stitch through the fabric so that the knot is on the top surface in an area that will be filled in with stitches, or on a paint line which will, of course, be covered with stitches later.

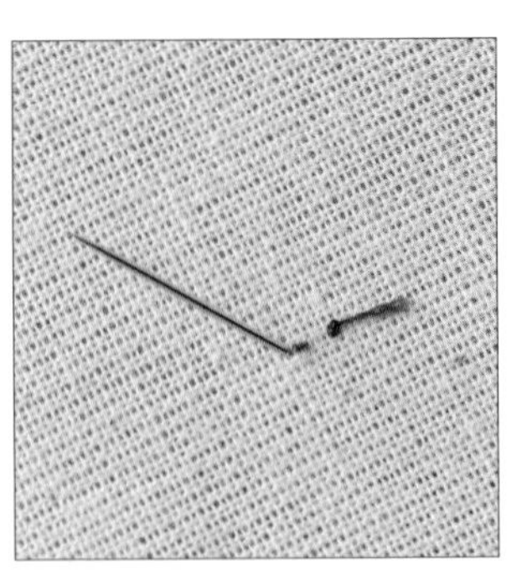

2 Make two small stab stitches into the same area either on or next to each other.

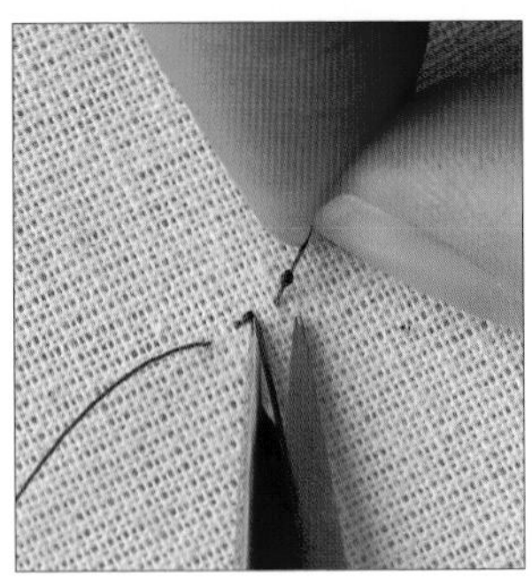

3 Carefully pull up the knot and cut it off. You are now ready to start stitching.

FINISHING A THREAD

To finish your thread you simply execute two more small stab stitches in the same way as you did at the start, working in an area which you know you are going to cover with embroidery later, or angle the stitches from underneath the embroidery that you have already created.

WORKING THREAD

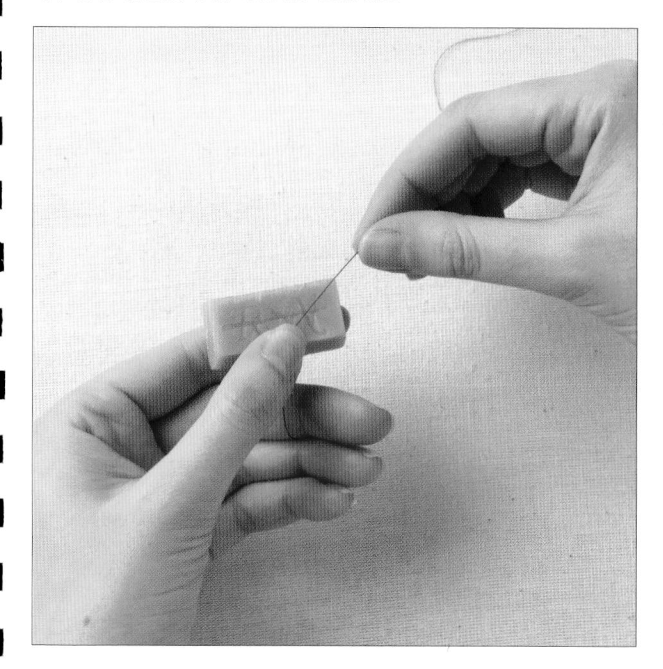

For gold embroidery, your working thread should always be run through beeswax to strengthen it and smooth off any loose fibres.

Always use a double thread to go through the centre of a thread (chips and cutwork) and a single thread to go over threads. This is because if your stitches are visible, you generally wish to see the gold rather than the holding stitch, unless you wish your holding stitches to be decorative, for example in the case of Or Nué (see page 80).

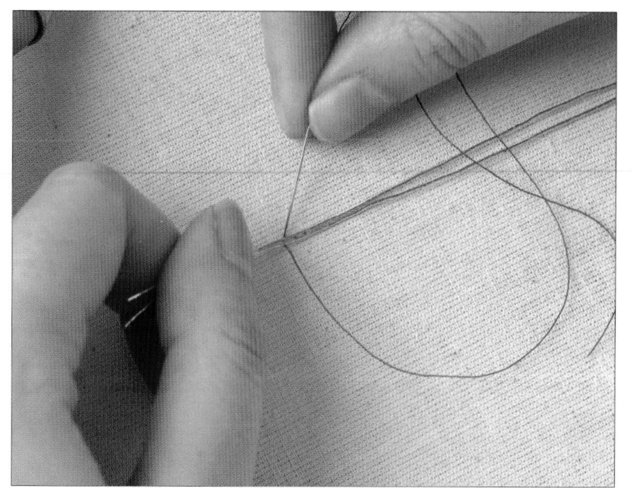

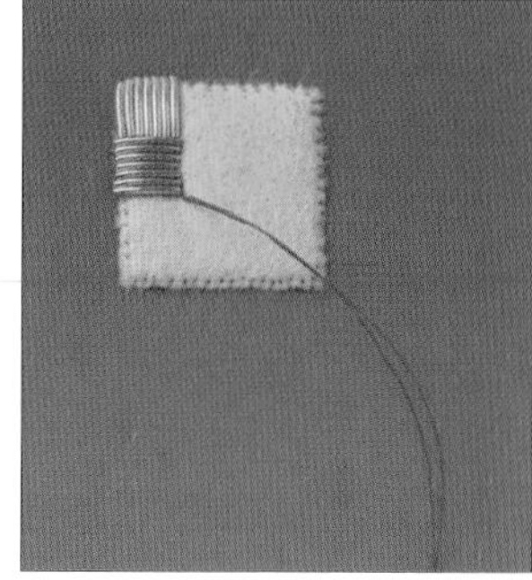

Use a double thread to go through the centre of a metal thread (chips and cutwork), as shown above, and a single thread to go over metal threads, shown on the left.

Order of work

There are often specified ways to plan your order of work depending on the techniques chosen. The order of work for metal thread embroidery is very important. The reason for this is that you need to build up your work, beginning with the padding and then stitching the most stable metal threads, and ending with the most delicate embroidery.

These two pages cover the order in which you would generally work a piece of metal thread embroidery.

1 Padding
The first stage is to attach any padding required for the raised areas of your embroidery. This could be felt or carpet-felt padding, soft or hard string or indeed a combination of any or all of the above depending on the desired effect. If your design is large, you may wish to stab stitch your paint lines prior to padding to ensure the fabrics do not pucker.

2 Kid and surface stitching
Any appliqué should be worked next, including kid, and it is also appropriate to add any decorative surface stitching at this stage as it tends to be closer to the face of the fabric than the metal thread. Working the surface stitching now also stops the embroidery threads catching on the metal and stretching it out of shape.

Marguerite Daisy
Helen McCook

Step 1: soft-string and craft-felt padding.

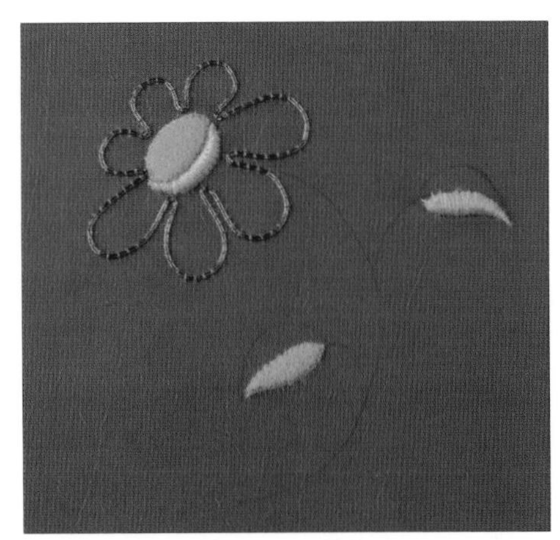

Step 2: couching is used to outline the petals.

3 Couching
Couching is done next, using Japanese thread, rococco, check, twist, Elizabethan twist or passing. You would also apply any pearl purl threads at this stage. This stage in the order of work is essentially to fill areas or to create outlines.

4 Cutwork
Cutwork can be worked using bright check, dull or wire check, smooth purl or rough purl. Techniques include chips (generally using bright, dull or wire check), cutwork, s-ing and s-ing with spangles.

5 Finishing touches
This is when you would complete the piece by adding embellishments in the form of beads or crystals, for example, or any additional surface stitching that needs to be placed after the goldwork has been executed.

Spring Flight (detail)
Helen McCook
Gilt metal threads, spangles and seed beads to silk ground.

Step 3: overstretched pearl purl with a coloured core is applied for the stem and leaf outlines. Spangles held down with beads embellish the flower centre.

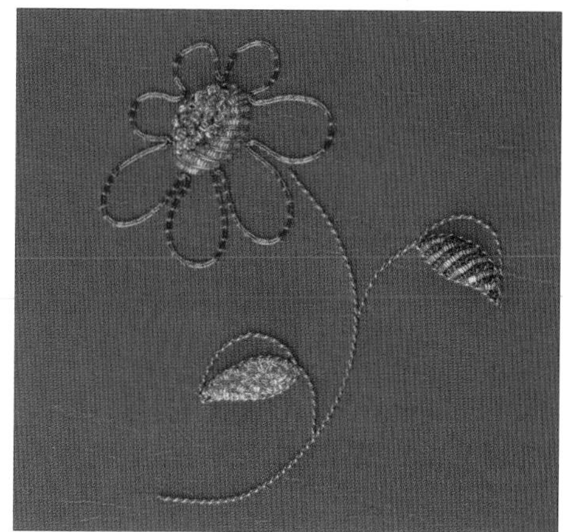

Step 4: chips and cutwork provide the finishing touches.

PADDING

People often seem inclined to hurry through the padding phase of goldwork, generally because they are so keen to move on to working with the metal threads themselves, but it is important to remember how key the padding stage is to achieving a good piece of metal thread work. A good analogy is this: if a house does not have good foundations, it will not stand well, and it is exactly the same with metal threads. If the padding is not strong, smooth and even enough then the metal threads will not lie evenly or be supported sufficiently, and this could lead to some of the metal threads cracking, which in turn will speed up the tarnishing process. It is therefore worth taking your time over this important process to ensure that your gold will be sufficiently cushioned.

Another reason to add a single layer of felt padding is to create a complementary coloured background on which to work chips or couching. This will blend the background into the colour of the stitching and make it less obvious if there are any tiny gaps.

Note

Don't rush your preparation.

Sample showing the padding stages of the 'Palais Pansy' by Helen McCook, working in soft string and craft felt.

SOFT-STRING PADDING

This type of padding is created to raise up and support cut goldwork and sometimes plate embroidery. Soft string, sometimes known as cotton bump (or bumph), is run through some beeswax and then cut to lengths which are longer than the designated shape to be filled by about 4cm (1½in) at each end. Ideally you want the length of the shape to be filled, and you also want to have sufficient numbers of threads to fill out the width at its widest point and to be a pleasing height. To ensure that you achieve this, cut the lengths as discussed above, and then twist them together and hold them in position over the shape to be worked. This will help you to have an idea of the height and width which will be left after the soft string has been stitched. Add more string until you are happy with the appearance.

Note

The beeswax which the soft string is gently run through is to help smooth off any fibres, but also to make the string more malleable and easier to mould if need be.

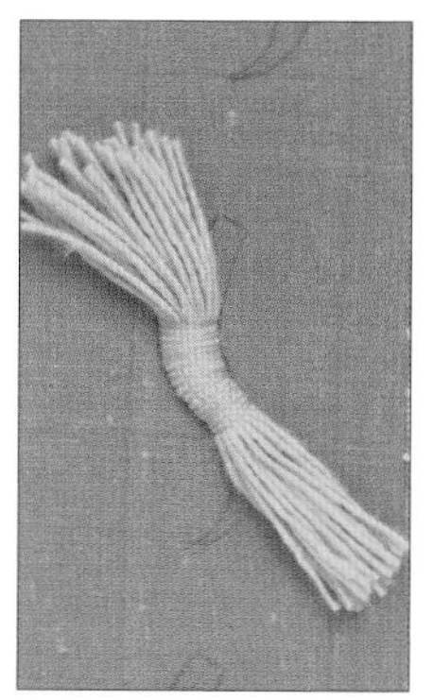

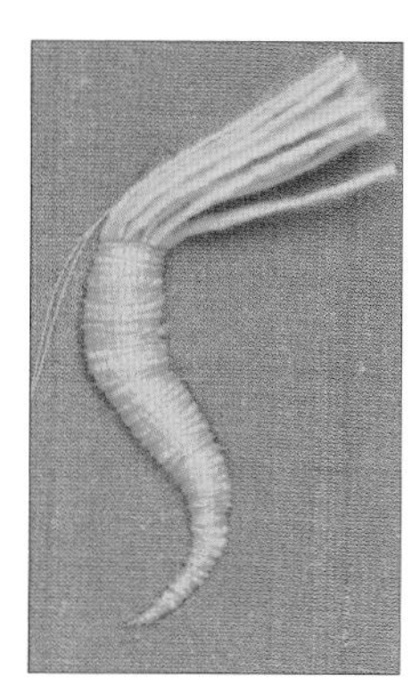

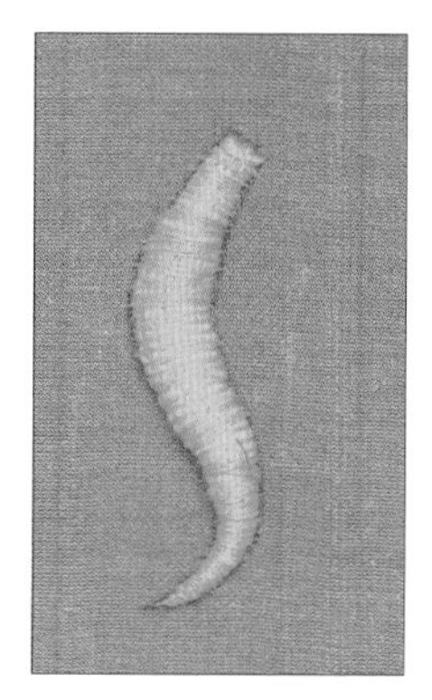

Soft-string padding, worked within a curved shape. If you are filling an irregular shape like this, always start stitching at the widest point. Use a waxed double thread to stitch the soft string down. To help you to determine how much soft string is needed to fill the widest parts of your chosen shape, and also to see how high the string padding will be, start by twisting the threads together gently. You will need to remember to untwist them when you start the stitching.

If you wish to taper the string towards a point then you will need to first lift the bulk of the soft string upwards from the face of the fabric. You will then need to separate out a few of the string lengths from the central underside and snip them away by placing the point of your scissors towards the point of the shape that you are working towards, and ensuring that the blades of the scissors are at approximately 45° to the base fabric. Smooth the remaining threads back over and keep stitching your way towards the end of the piece. By snipping a few lengths at a time from the underside you will find it easier to achieve a gently tapering, smooth-surfaced piece of soft-string padding, and by the time you come to the end of the shape you need only snip off the excess soft string at the appropriate angle and stitch it down.

Note

See also the section on cutwork over soft-string padding, on pages 62–63.

HARD-STRING PADDING

Hard string is used as the base over which to stitch couched metal threads to form patterns. These patterns can take the form of chevrons, diamonds, stripes and so on, or can be more complex, in which case they are known as basketweave (see page 56).

When using gold, it is advisable to soften the harsh white appearance of the string by dyeing it, generally using tea. Once it is dry, run it gently through some beeswax to help make it a little more malleable. If you are using silver, the string can be left undyed.

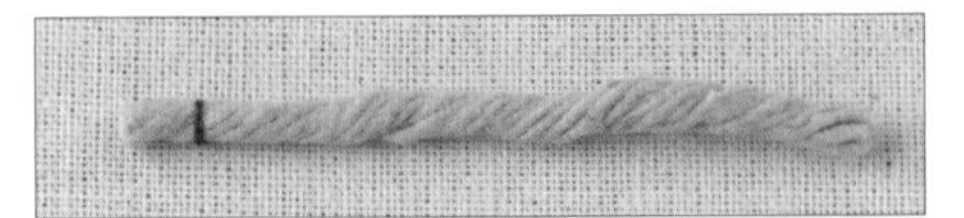

1 To start this technique, begin your thread using the waste-knot technique (see page 34) in an area which will be covered.

2 When executing the couching, place your stitches at a distance of approximately 3mm (⅛in) apart.

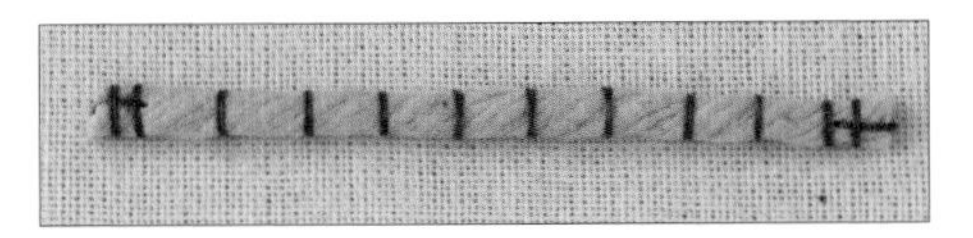

3 Ensure that you finish the ends of the string by putting a stitch from the fabric at the very end of the string and going down into the string itself.

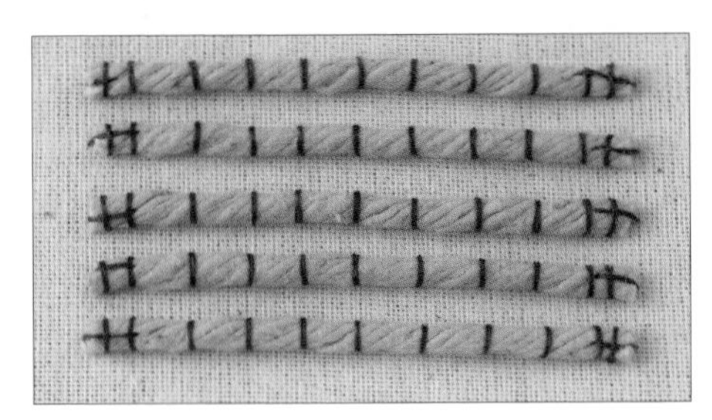

4 Couch lengths of hard string down securely and carefully, ensuring that they lie in straight, parallel lines (for basketweave) or in whatever configuration suits your design. Make sure that the distances between the pieces of string are even. Generally this should be between one and a half and two times the width of the string, depending on the desired effect and design.

FELT PADDING

Felt padding can consist of one layer or multiple layers of felt in a colour which complements the chosen metal: yellow for gold, white or light grey for silver and brown for copper or bronze. If there are multiple layers of felt to build up a slightly higher shape, then the smallest piece of felt is stitched down first and the largest is stitched down last (see page 42). This is so that the external finish is smooth rather than stepped, which would be the resulting appearance if the largest were stitched down first and the smallest last.

To ensure that you have achieved the correct size of felt for your shape, you could place your design on a light box, trace it through the felt and then trim it off. Alternatively, you could use a copy of the design to create a template which can then be pinned on to the felt and cut round, or you could use prick and pounce to transfer the design (see page 32).

Tudor Rose

First-year apprenticeship goldwork embroidery by Helen McCook, executed in a variety of golden metal threads and silk floss to linen ground, showing felt and hard-string padding.

Applying multiple layers of felt

1 To start stitching, thread a needle with Gutermann thread in a complementary colour to your felt and metal threads. Use the waste-knot technique to start your thread (see page 34). Bring your needle up in the fabric and take it down into the edge of your first piece of felt at a slight angle (about 45° to your base fabric). This will make a small stitch on the top surface of the felt that will pick up more of the felt as you move through it. Stitch all the way around the piece leaving gaps of about 1.5–2cm (5/8–3/4in) depending on the size of the piece of felt. This will secure your felt in place.

2 You then need to go back around your shape, filling in more stitches with a gap of no more than 2 to 3mm (about 1/8in) between them.

3 Once the whole shape is held down like this, you then either add the next (larger) layer of felt or you can finish off the thread by executing two more tiny stab stitches on or next to each other, either in a nearby area which you know will be covered or angled out slightly from underneath the newly applied felt.

4 Add a third layer, following the same method, if required.

CARPET-FELT PADDING

Whilst a fair amount of height can be achieved by using layers of felt, in order to create a higher, more sculptural effect it is worth considering the use of carpet felt. In this instance it is best to utilise a copy of your original design to use as a template which you can pin to the carpet felt and cut around. The largest piece of carpet felt should be fractionally smaller all round in size than the painted or drawn outline for the shape. Before stitching the carpet felt you should chamfer the edge. Do this by holding your scissor blades so they lie flat to the side of the felt at an angle of approximately 45° and effectively cut off the top corner of the felt.

1 The largest piece of carpet felt is stitched down first using a waxed double thread. begin by laying herringbone or cross stitching over the piece in order to secure it in place (carpet felt is very easily broken down by stitching directly into it). If you are working with a substantial piece of carpet felt or are working an unusual shape which will need definition, then you should now gently work long-and-short stitch along the edge of the carpet-felt padding.

2 If there are any additional smaller layers you should stitch these in order from the largest to the smallest, having first chamfered (shaped) the edges by angling your scissors to cut or round off the top corner on the edge of the felt. The reason for chamfering is to help create a smooth overall shape by easing the edges of the separate pieces of carpet felt together. You may also need to long-and-short the edge on these additional layers.

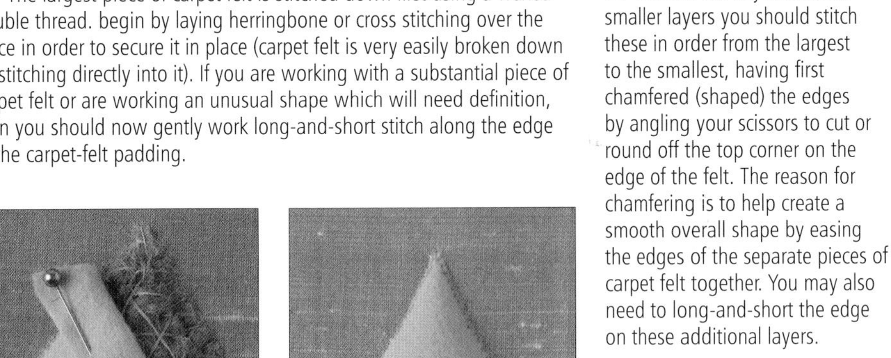

3 Having stitched all of the required layers of carpet felt, apply a single layer of craft felt over the top using exactly the same technique as that used to attach felt padding (described opposite). This layer of felt will help to trap in all the fibrous matter from the carpet felt and provide a smooth surface to settle the gold against. It should be a complementary colour to your chosen metal.

Methods

There are many options that may be used in combination with each other to create a seemingly endless array of appearances in metal thread work. This section explores the most commonly used of these.

COUCHING

Couching is the most commonly used way of filling areas of your chosen design with metal thread. There are a number of different ways of doing this, depending on how you decide to lay your threads and where you decide to plunge your ends. The type, colour and size of threads also drastically alter the appearance and light play with this technique. In the following sections, the couching methods used for various metal threads are discussed. A single waxed machine thread or strand of stranded cotton is the most common choice of sewing thread with which to make the couching stitches, however any thread that is relatively stable and even in width can be used.

COMBINING THREADS

Using combinations of threads, for example rococco, Japanese gold, passing, check and twist, when couching will help you to achieve different effects. Each of these may be stitched at a variety of angles. These threads, in a range of sizes, colours and directions, can be used to create different textures and to alter the play of light across the surface of the work.

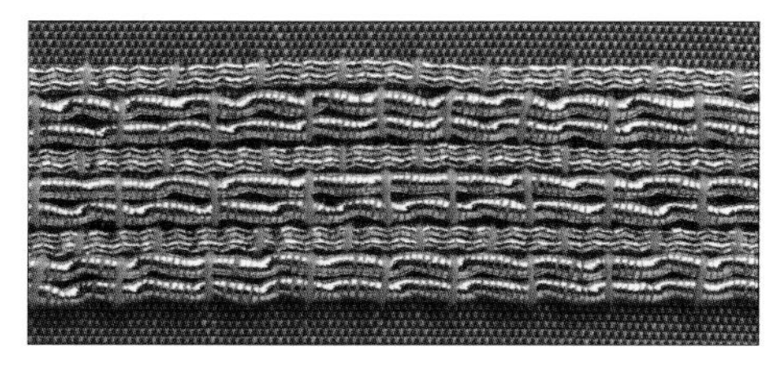

Different sizes of gold rococco and silver check couched down in pairs in parallel rows.

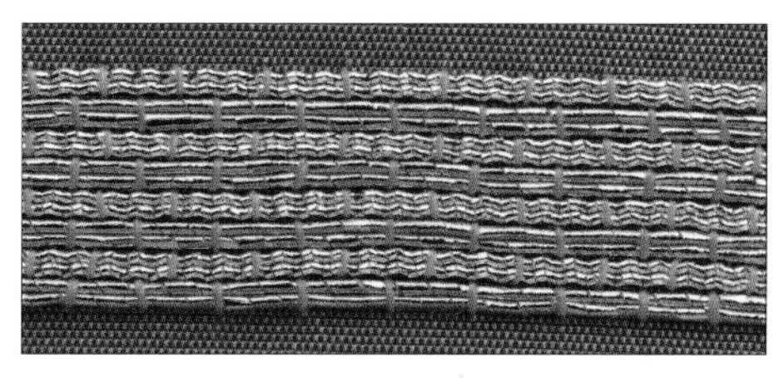

Japanese gold threads couched down in pairs alternating with pairs of silver check strands.

Japanese gold threads alternating with silver twist, both worked in pairs.

Silver twist couched down in pairs alternating with pairs of gold rococco.

***Snowdrops* (detail)**

Helen McCook

Worked in silver, gilt and coloured metal threads, spangles, assorted shades of stranded cotton threads, seed beads and diamanté to silk dupion ground.

JAPANESE GOLD

Japanese gold is stitched down in pairs. Either use two reels and leave the threads on the reel, or cut off an appropriate length of thread and fold it in half. Start your stitching 4–5cm (1½–2in) from one end of the gold threads.

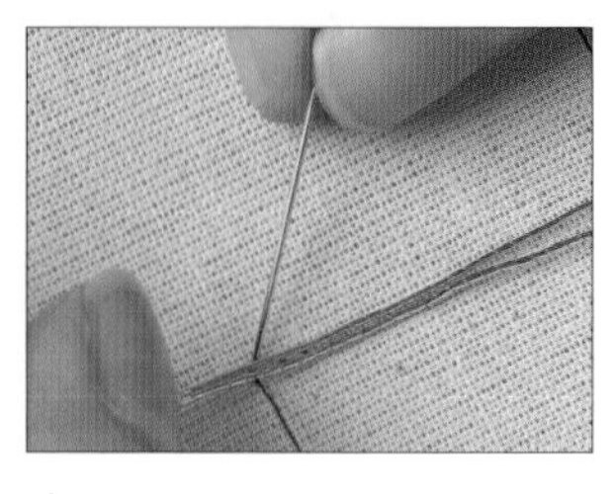

1 Take the first stitch over the gold threads, ensuring it is at 90° to the threads. Avoid pulling the stitch too tight – it should be tight enough to hold the gold securely but not so tight that it dents the threads.

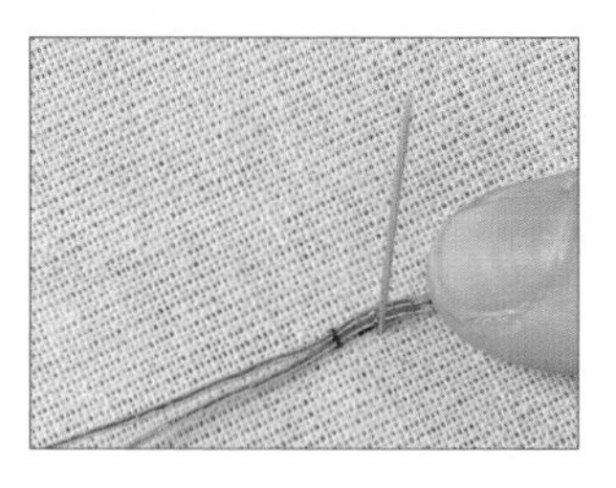

2 Pull the needle through and position it ready for the next stitch. Stitches should usually be approximately 3–4mm (¼in) apart, but this depends on the pattern.

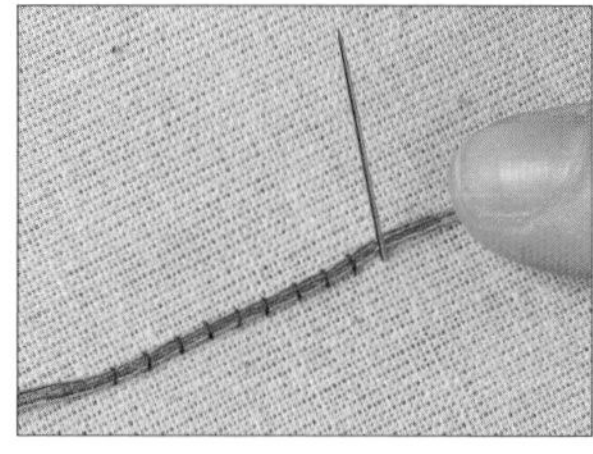

3 Continue to stitch along the gold thread, ensuring the stitches are evenly spaced and all lie at 90° to the threads. Make sure the gold threads don't twist over as you work, and do not over-tighten the stitches.

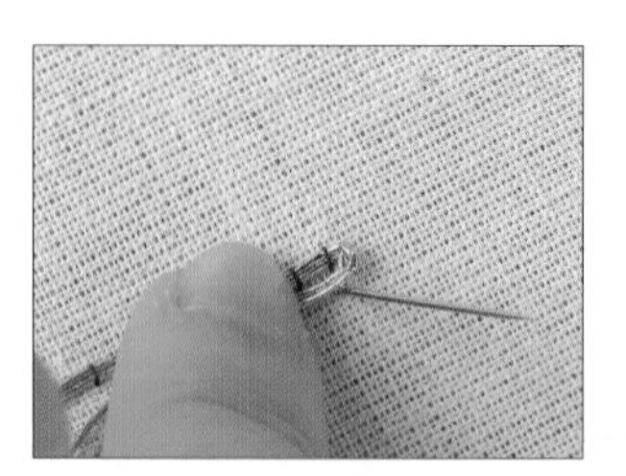

4 To turn the gold thread back through 180°, first bend the thread back on itself. Hold the gold threads firmly in place, and bring the needle up on the outer side of the threads in the second row, just below the last stitch.

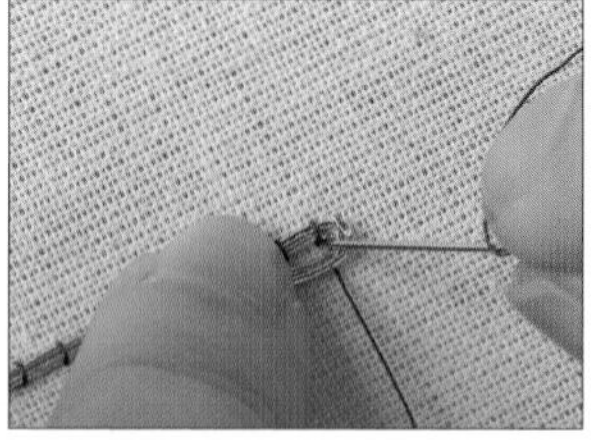

5 Take the needle down through the hole at the end of the last stitch.

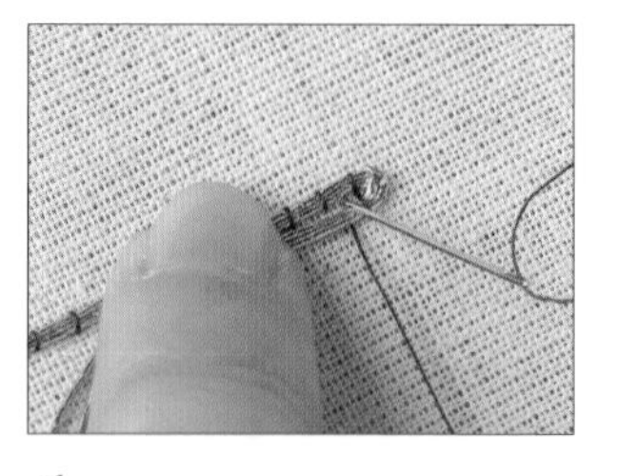

6 Tighten the stitch, making sure the two pairs of gold threads are still lying parallel, and make the next stitch halfway between the last two stitches of the previous row.

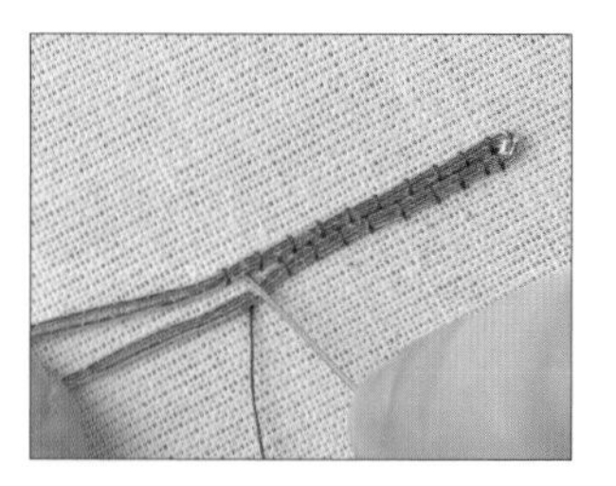

7 Continue working along the gold threads, placing the stitches in between those of the previous row, in a brickwork pattern (see page 50). When you have finished couching, take the thread through to the back of the work ready for fastening off (see opposite).

Note

When couching adjacent rows of gold, always work from the outer to the inner edge, and angle the needle underneath the previous row to help pull the two rows of gold threads together neatly.

TURNING AND PLUNGING

Just as there are a variety of ways to fill shapes with couching, so too there are a few ways of turning. The one shown opposite is probably the most commonly used, but two methods for turning around corners and angles are given on pages 48 and 49.

This is also a good time to mention plunging. The threads which we use for couching can tend to fray so they need to be secured. The most aesthetically pleasing way of doing this is to plunge the ends individually through to the back of the fabric, oversew them and snip off the excess thread to create a neat finish.

Plunging and fastening off

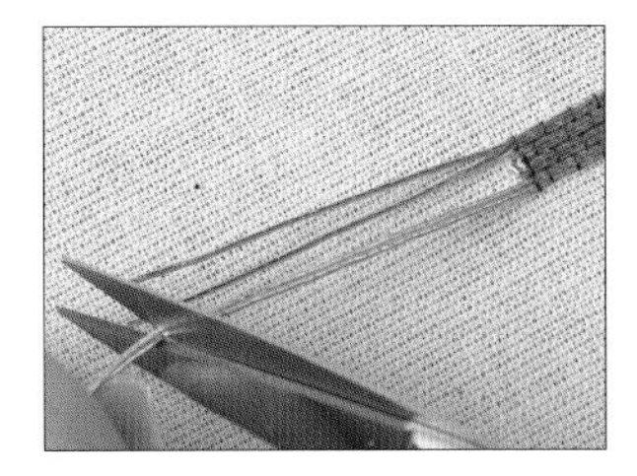

1 When you have finished couching, cut off the gold threads so that the tails are the same length as those at the start.

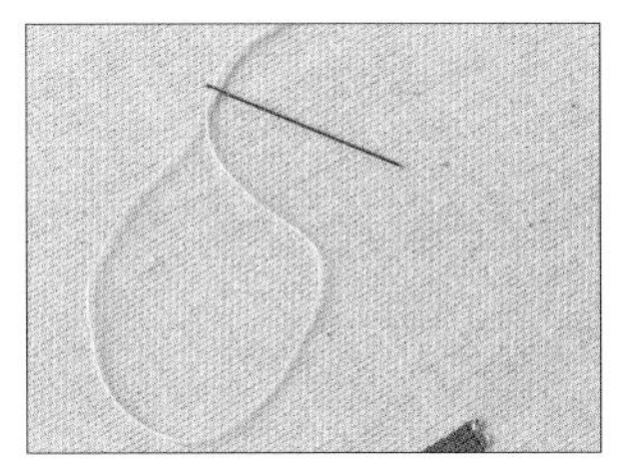

2 Take a bigger needle and pass the two ends of a length of buttonhole thread through it to form a loop.

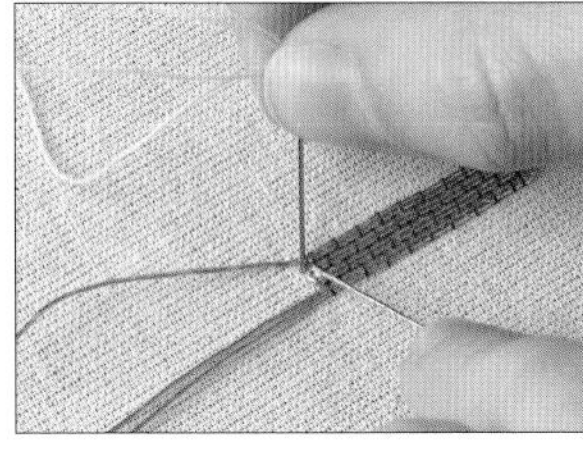

3 Lift the gold threads out of the way and insert the needle where you wish to plunge them.

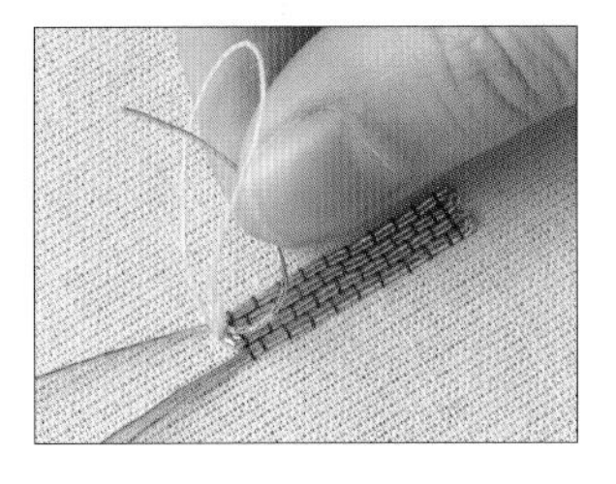

4 Pull the thread through, leaving a loop on the surface. Pass the end of one of the gold threads through the loop.

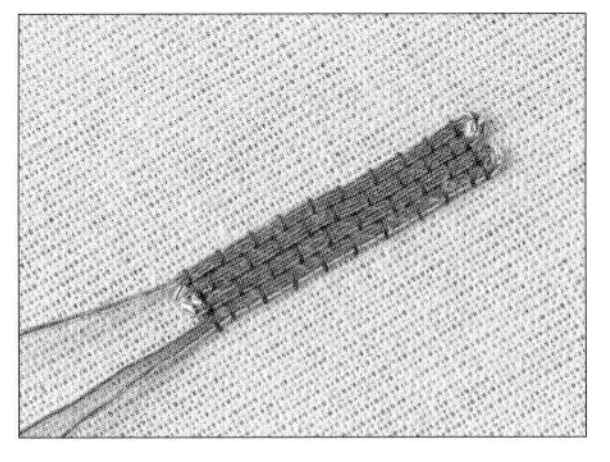

5 Pull the loop through. Ensure the end of the gold thread is not too close to the loop, otherwise it could be damaged. As you tighten the loop, the gold thread will be pulled through to the back.

6 Repeat for the remaining gold threads.

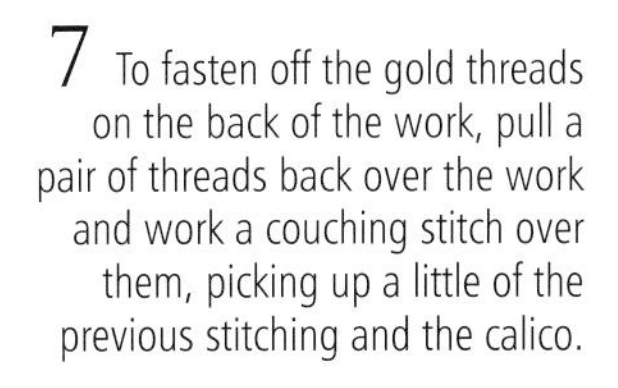

7 To fasten off the gold threads on the back of the work, pull a pair of threads back over the work and work a couching stitch over them, picking up a little of the previous stitching and the calico.

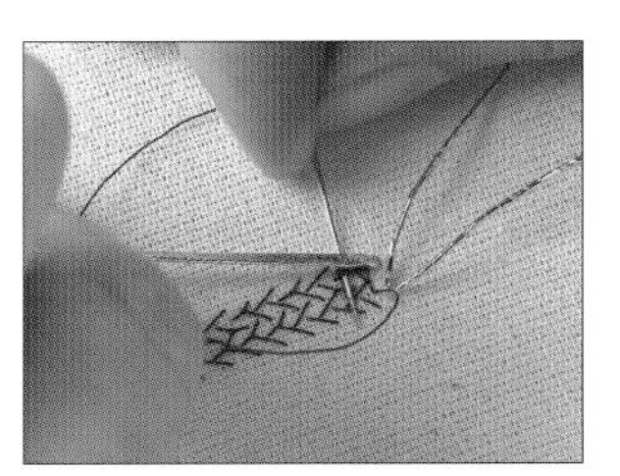

Note

Some people prefer to use a curved needle to fasten the ends off at the back of their work. You should try both a straight and a curved needle and decide which one works best for you.

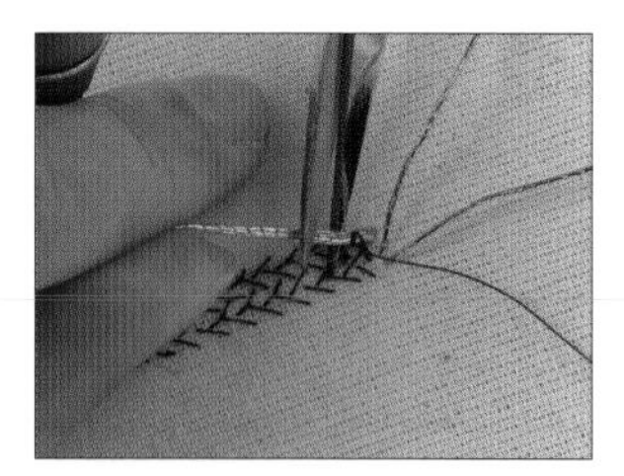

8 Work three or four more stitches over the top of the first and cut off the tails.

9 Finish the remaining gold threads in the same way.

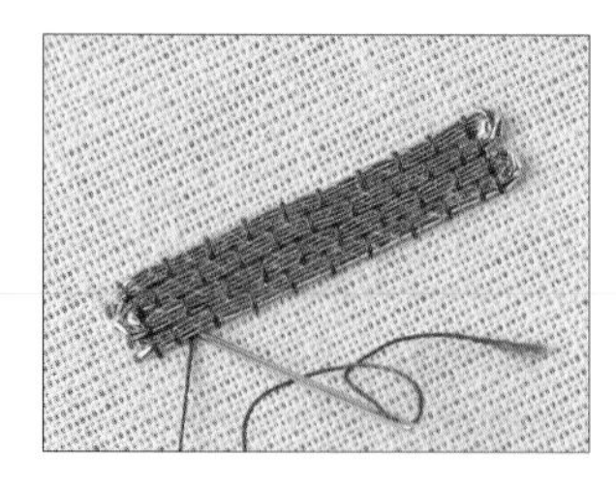

10 Take the sewing thread through to the front and make a tiny stitch at the edge of the work, angling the needle underneath the gold.

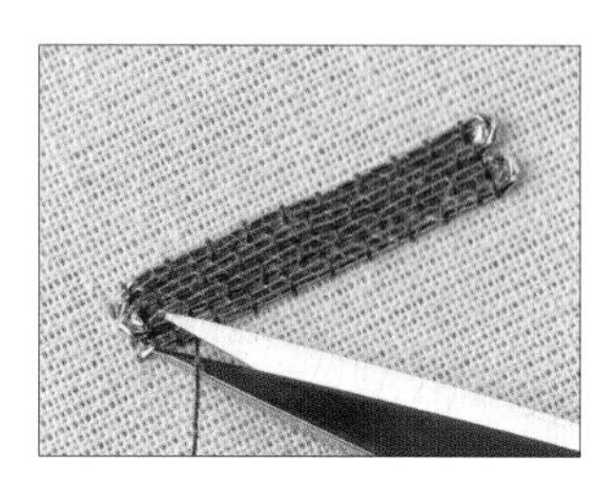

11 Make two further stitches in the same place, bring the needle through to the front and cut off the thread close to the fabric.

Couching around a right-angled corner

1 Having couched the gold threads to the corner, turn the gold threads through 90°. Bring the needle up on the corner and work a diagonal stitch across it.

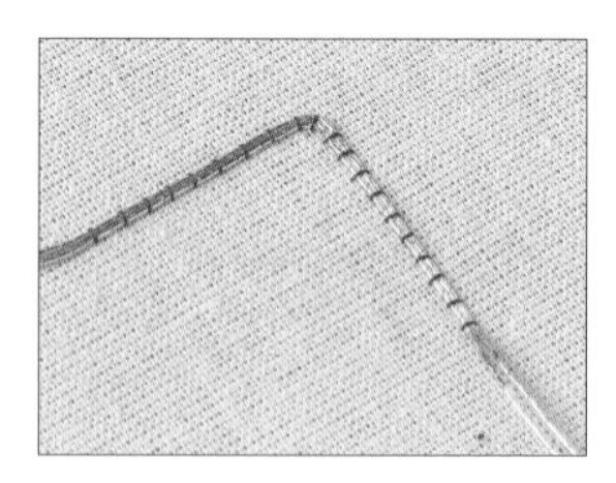

2 Continue couching, positioning the stitches so they match those on the first side of the right angle.

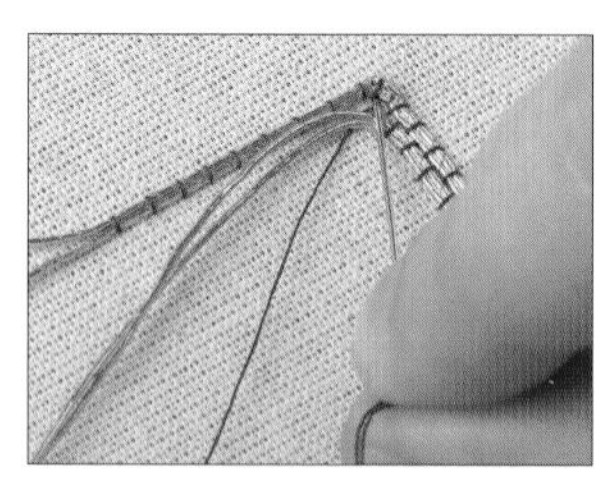

3 Turn the gold through 180° to encourage it to bend (see page 46) and work back towards the corner. At the corner, make a diagonal stitch. Bring the needle up on the outside edge and take it down through the same hole as the first diagonal stitch, angling the needle underneath the first pair of gold threads as you do so to help keep the row together.

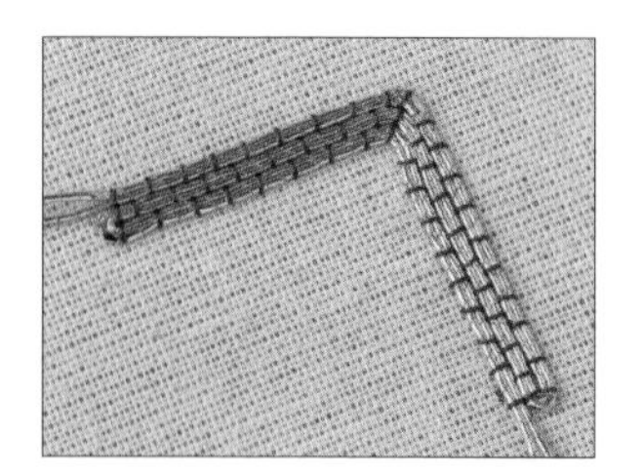

4 Continue couching in the same way, turning the gold at the end of each row and making sure the diagonal stitches at the corner are aligned, as shown.

Fishtailing around an acute angle

It is difficult to make a sharp corner by the usual plunging method, so acute angles are worked by plunging the ends of the threads in a fishtail arrangement.

1 Couch down a pair of gold threads. When you reach the corner, cut off the ends, leaving long tails for plunging later. Lay a second line of gold threads across the first, creating a 'V' shape. Couch it down, starting just above the crossing point and aligning the stitches with those in the first row.

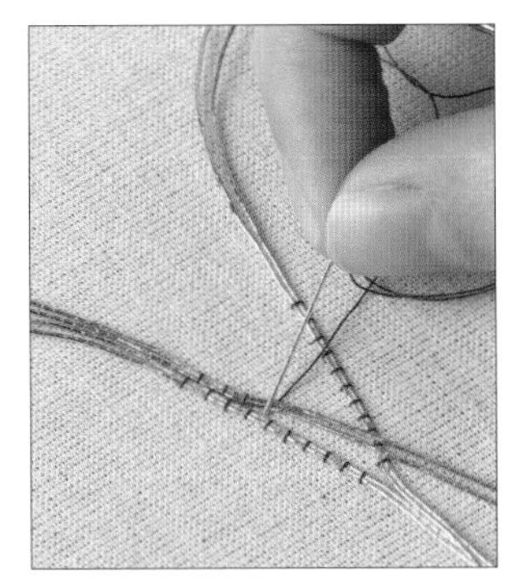

2 Cut off the gold threads, leaving long tails as before, and lay another pair alongside the first, inside the 'V'. Couch the threads down, taking the stitches over from the outer to the inner edge and angling the needle underneath the first row to draw the two rows together. Lay the couching stitches in a brickwork pattern (see pages 46 and 50).

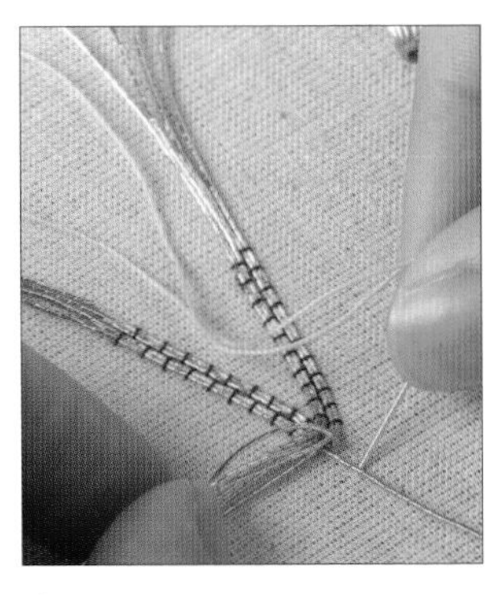

3 Continue to lay pairs of gold threads in this way. When you have finished, lift all the gold threads out of the way apart from the first pair. Plunge these through to the back (see page 47).

4 Plunge the second pair of gold threads just above the first pair.

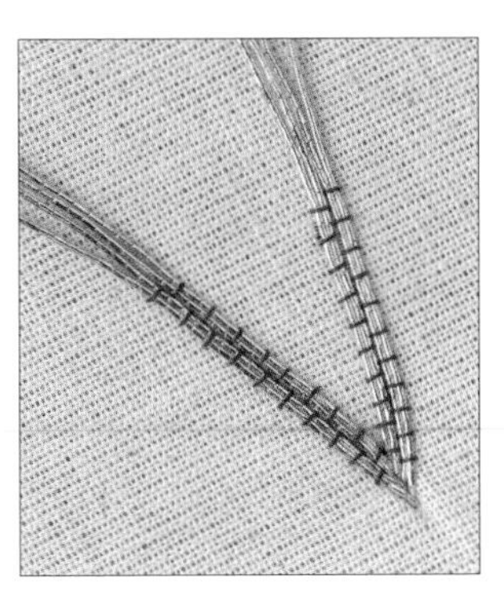

5 Continue in this way, plunging the pairs of threads in the order in which they were worked, and each time taking them through at a point just above the previous threads, as shown.

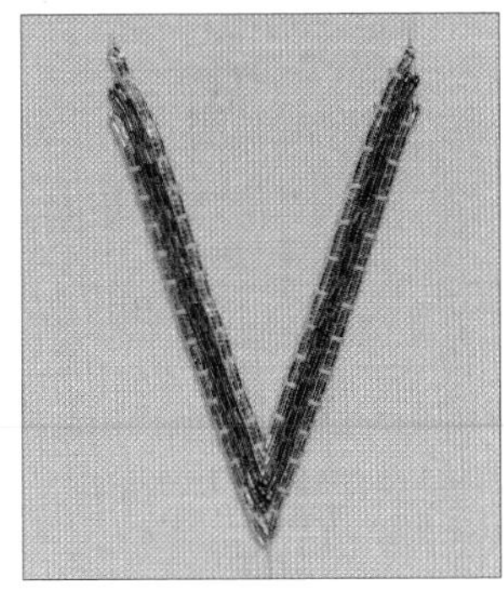

An interesting effect can be achieved by couching down different coloured metal threads in a 'V' shape. Here, pairs of gold, copper and silver threads have been couched down using bricking (see page 50).

BRICKING

Bricking is the most common method for holding down the couched threads. If it has been executed correctly, it creates a firm, stable embroidery with a beautifully even finish. The stitches should be evenly spaced, sit at 90° to the metal thread which they are holding down, and all be pulled to the same tension so that none of them lie higher or lower on the gold's surface than the others. However, even where a pattern has been worked well, the odd rogue stitch can often be overlooked. Bearing in mind that the human eye is trained to pick up patterns, it is important to point out that the single rogue stitch will always be the one that the eye is drawn to even when all the others are perfect.

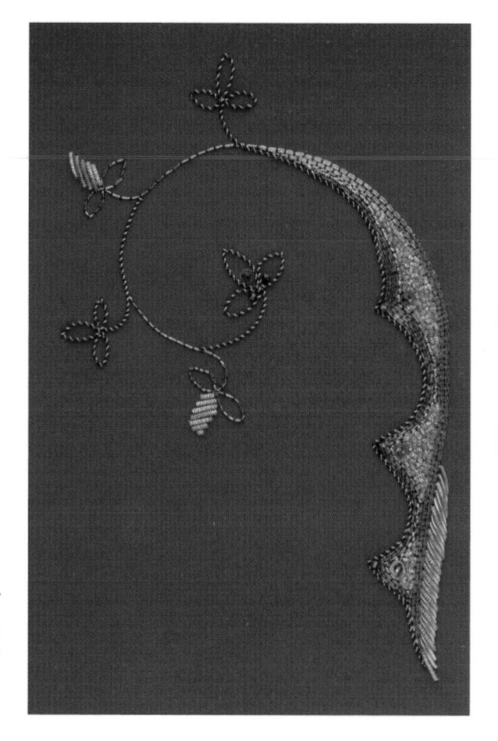

Crozier Border
Helen McCook
Inspired by the Lutrell Psalter, worked in couching, flat and raised cutwork, pearl purl, chips, spangles and beads.

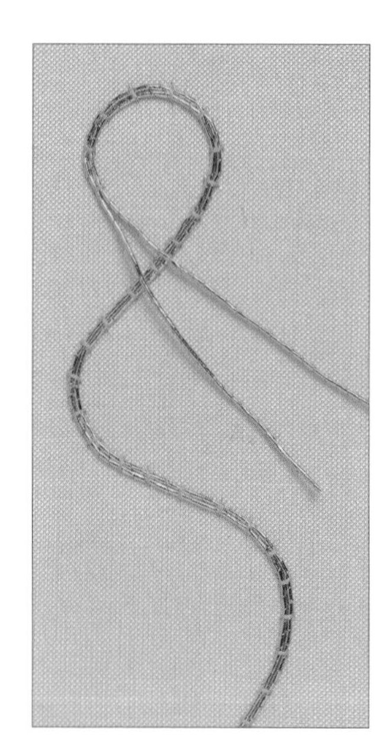

First row of bricking pairs of gold thread in a curve.

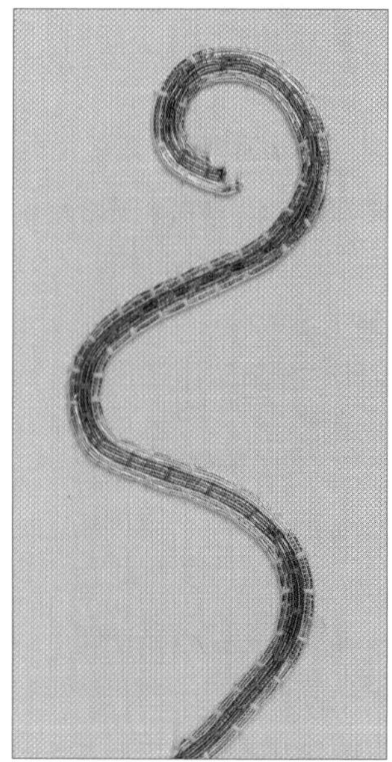

Two further rows added, using pairs of copper and silver threads.

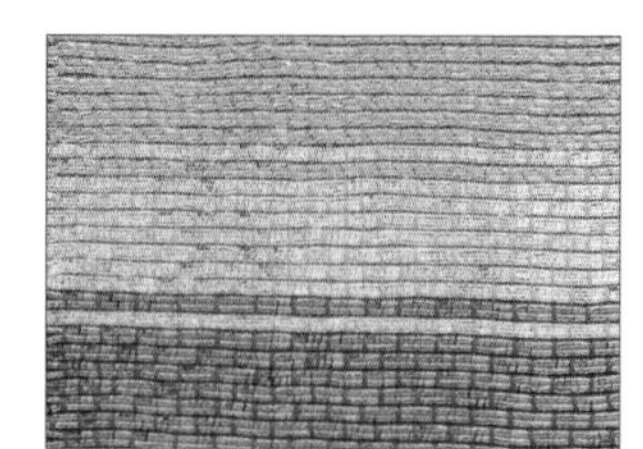

Here, bricking has been used with different coloured metal threads couched to create a strong design.

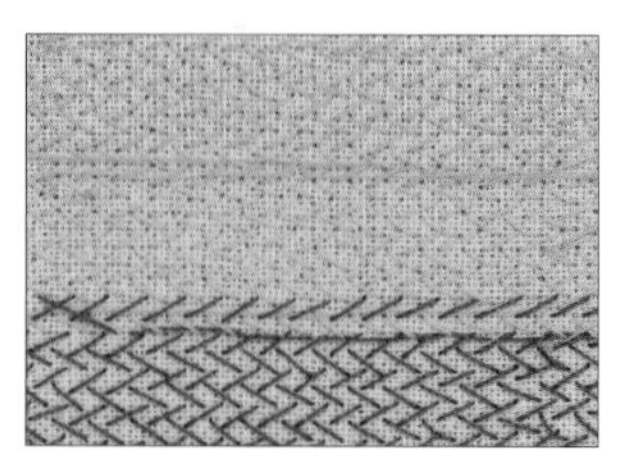

The back of the design reveals the nature of the stitching.

COUCHING IN A CIRCLE

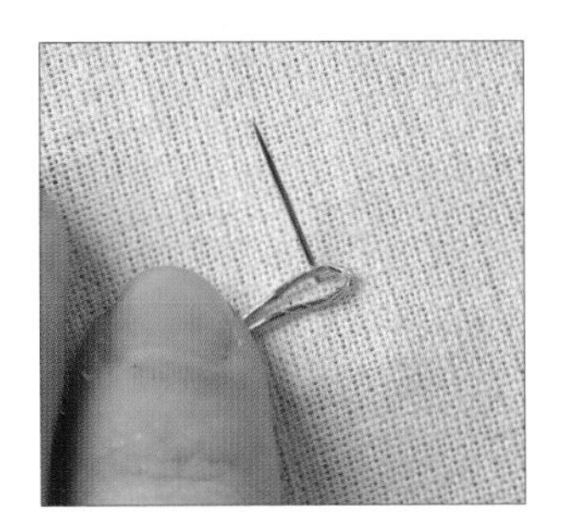

1 Create a fold in the gold and lay a stitch over it to form the centre of the circle. Bring the needle back through at the edge of the gold, approximately 3–4mm (¼in) away from the first stitch.

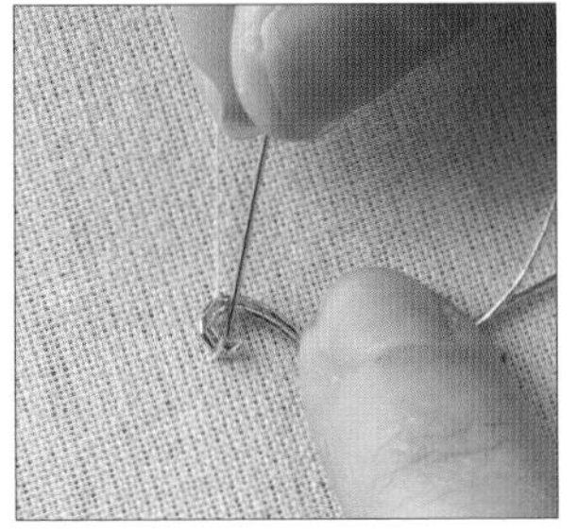

2 Make the second stitch over both threads, then bend the gold back on itself to form a tight curve. Stitch over the top of the curve, bringing the needle through on the outer edge of the gold and angling it back down under the gold you attached in step 1.

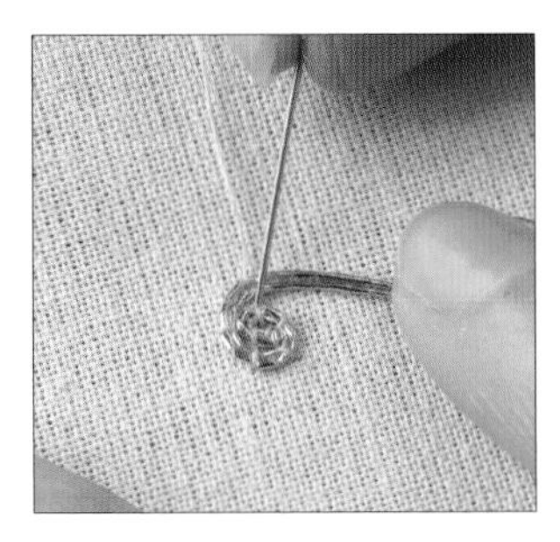

3 Continue stitching the gold in a tight circle, working the stitches from the outside of the circle in towards the centre and angling the needle underneath the previously worked gold threads. Ensure that all the stitches are evenly spaced and placed at 90° to the gold.

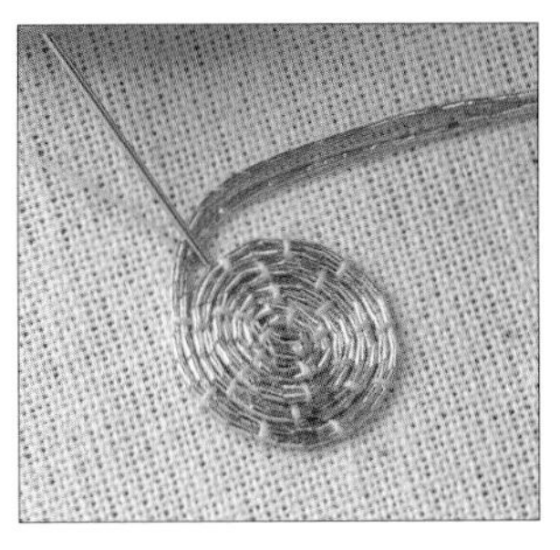

4 As the circle grows, make sure it maintains a good shape and does not distort, and that the gold threads lie flat and parallel without twisting.

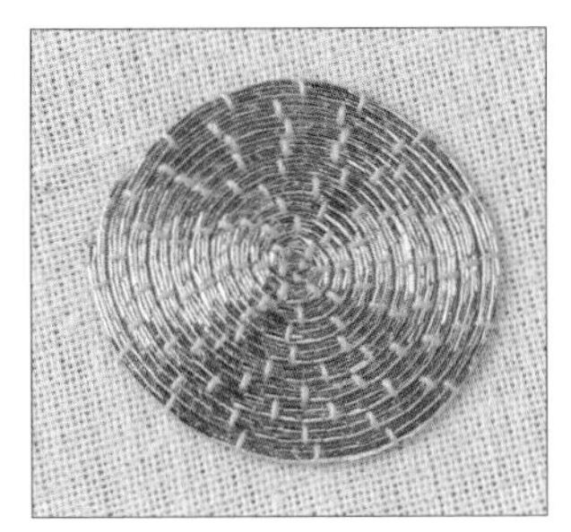

5 When the circle is the desired size, plunge the gold threads through to the back of the work.

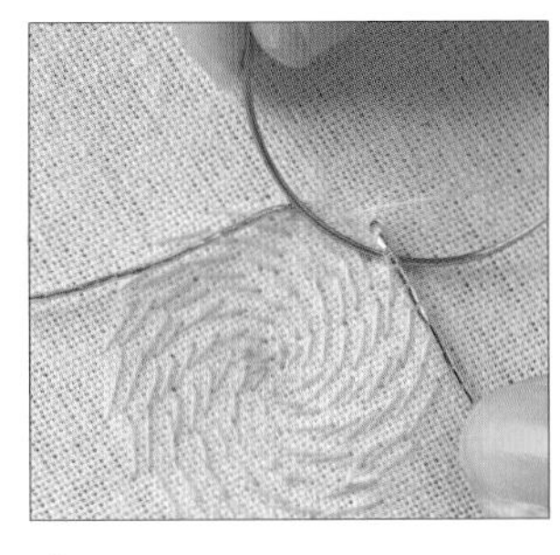

6 Bend the gold threads back on themselves and oversew them firmly in place on the back of the work using either a curved or a straight needle, whichever you are more comfortable with. Trim off the excess gold to finish.

PEARL PURL

Pearl purl can be used in lines of couching or overstretched and wrapped with a coloured thread as its core, but it is generally used to create lines or to outline areas. When overstretching, you want to achieve an even pull across the entire length so that the individual twists in the metal appear at regular intervals. The central core can be anything you wish it to be – stranded cottons, silks, chenille threads or even other metals – as long as they sit comfortably in the twist of the pearl purl.

Note

Although pearl purl does not fray and can be snipped off when you have finished with it, the central core will probably be a thread that will fray. You will therefore need to plunge it and fasten off at the back as you would with some of the other couching threads (see page 47).

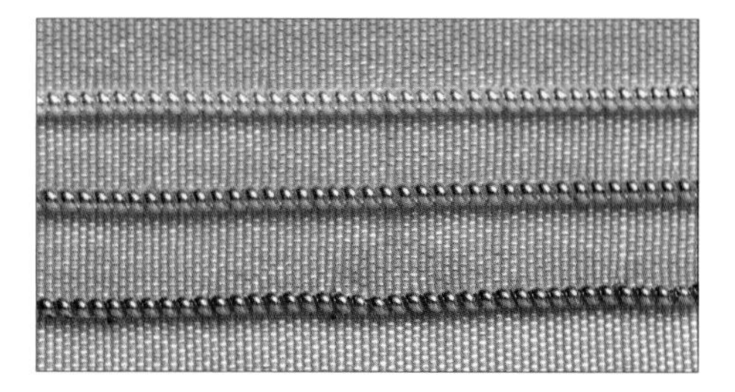

Pearl purl.

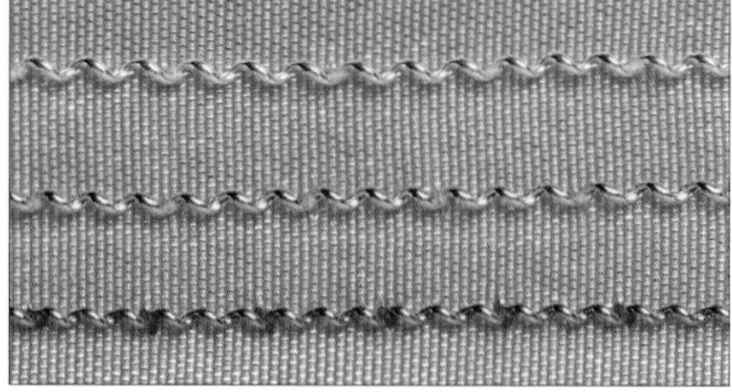

Overstretched pearl purl.

Overstretched pearl purl with a coloured core.

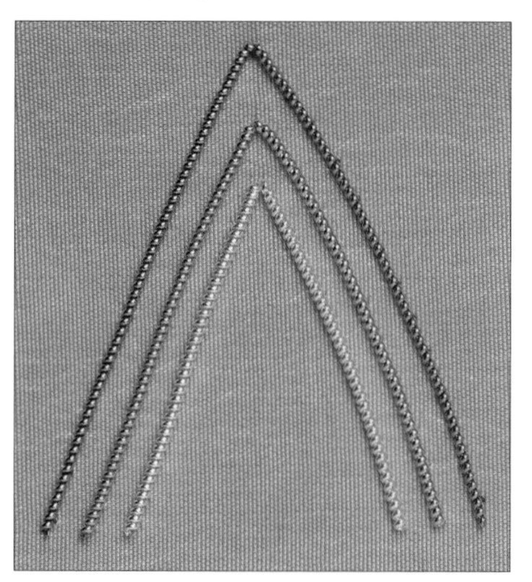

Pearl purl worked in an inverted 'V' shape.

Stretching pearl purl

Before using pearl purl, you need to stretch it slightly to loosen the coils. This allows the thread with which you attach the pearl purl to sit comfortably between the coils. Do not confuse this with overstretched pearl purl (see above), which is used to produce very different effects.

A comparison of unstretched pearl purl (top) with stretched pearl purl (bottom).

Attaching pearl purl

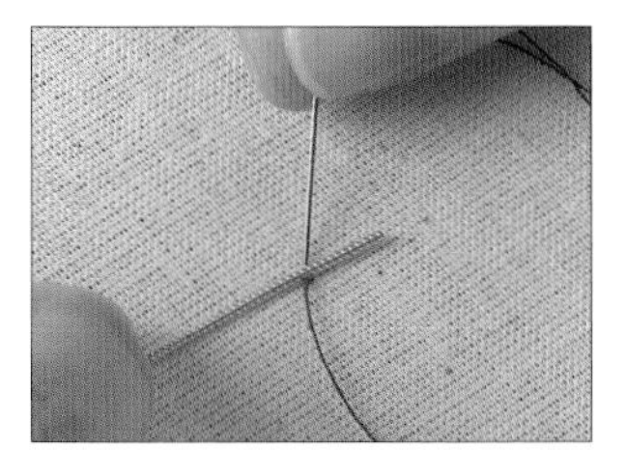

1 Bring the thread to the front and take it over the pearl purl, about 1cm (½in) from the end.

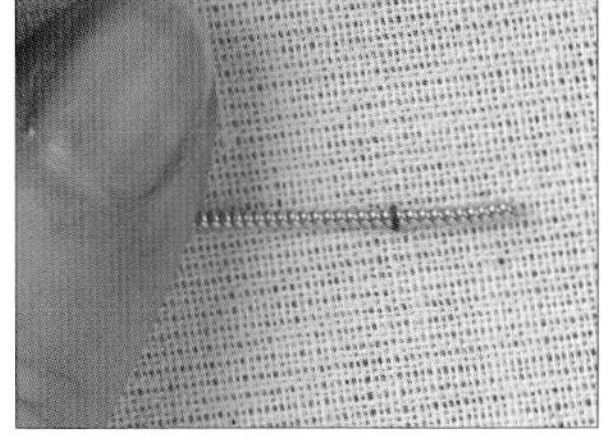

2 Pull the thread tight to form the stitch. Here, the stitch is lying on top on the pearl purl and is clearly visible.

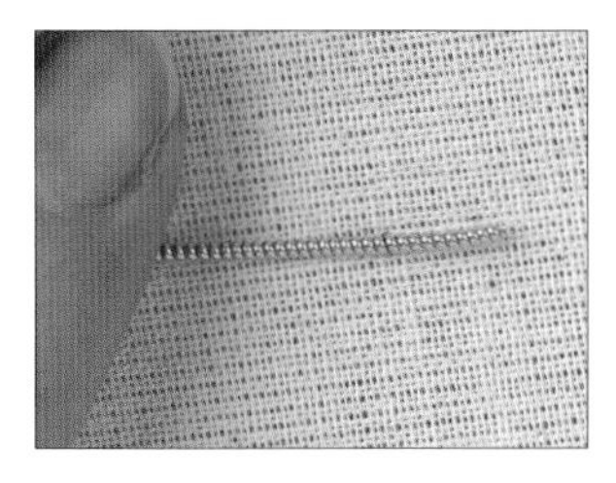

3 Here the stitch has been pulled down so that it 'pops' between the coils and becomes invisible – this is the correct way to attach pearl purl.

Note

For clarity, I have used a thread of contrasting colour with which to attach the pearl purl in this demonstration. In reality it is best to use a self-coloured (matching) thread to work pearl purl.

Turning pearl purl into a circle

1 If necessary, twist the pearl purl to position the first stitch approximately 1cm (½in) from the end. Continue stitching, bringing the needle up underneath the pearl purl and taking it down as close as possible to (but not through) the same hole.

Note

Pearl purl is very springy, so you will need to push it into a circle shape as you work.

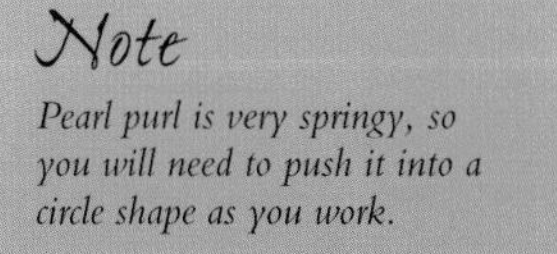

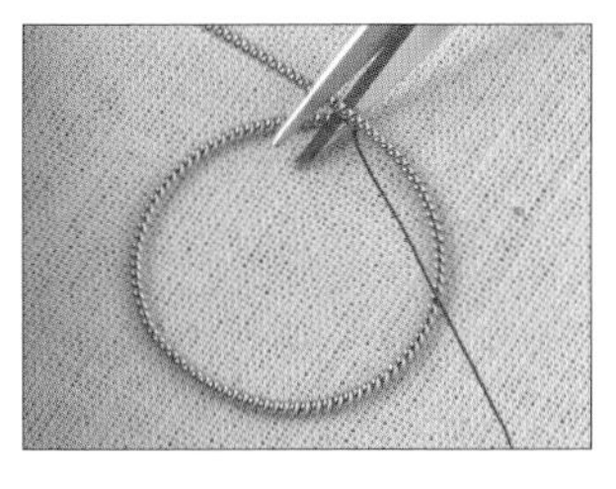

2 When the circle is complete, snip off the pearl purl so that the two ends meet but do not overlap.

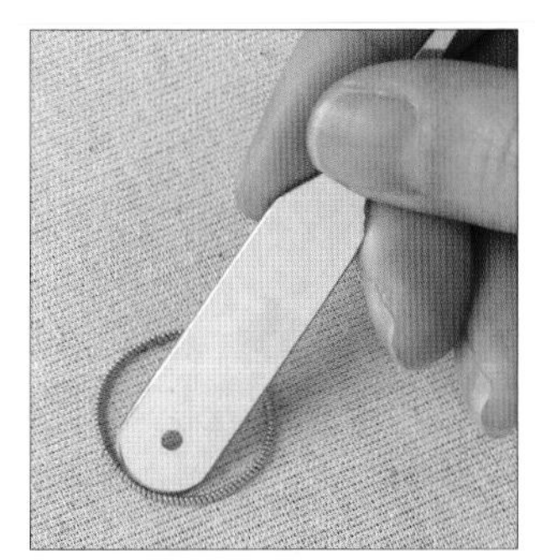

3 Place the final stitch over the end of the pearl purl and pinch the ends together using a pair of tweezers so that you cannot see the join.

4 Refine the shape of the circle using the round end of a mellor to eliminate any kinks in the pearl purl.

TWISTS

Twists can be stitched down in pairs using the couching technique or they may be stitched down in individual strands that require an invisible stitch. The latter technique is demonstrated below. To show the technique clearly I have used a thread of contrasting colour, but you would normally use a self-coloured (matching) thread to couch down twist so that you do not see any of the holding stitches.

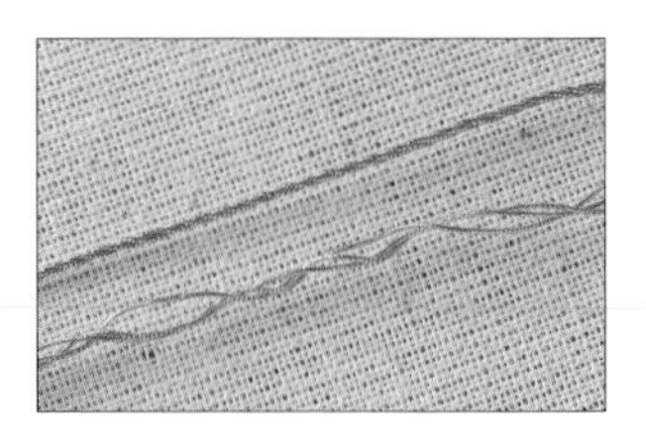

3-ply twist consists of three strands – the top thread is normal 3-ply twist and the bottom thread is 3-ply twist unravelled.

Elizabethan twist

Elizabethan twist is a small-scale twist thread which is generally used in conjunction with a coloured thread to fill small areas with gold and a decorative pattern at the same time. An example of Elizabethan twist used in this way is provided by the small leaves on the Tudor Rose, shown on page 41.

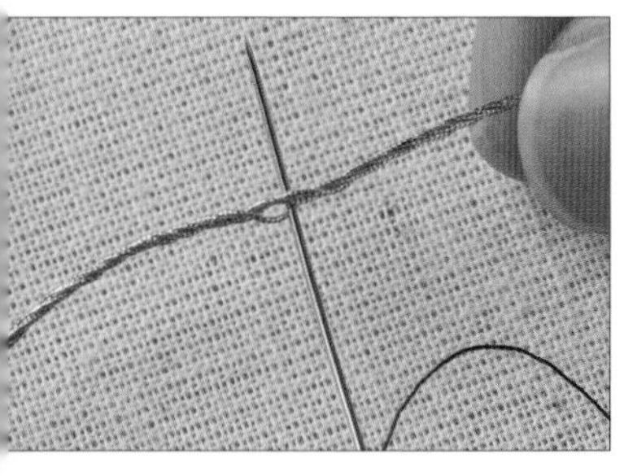

1 To start off the sewing thread, bring it up through the fabric and pass it through the twist – over the bottom strand and under the top two strands.

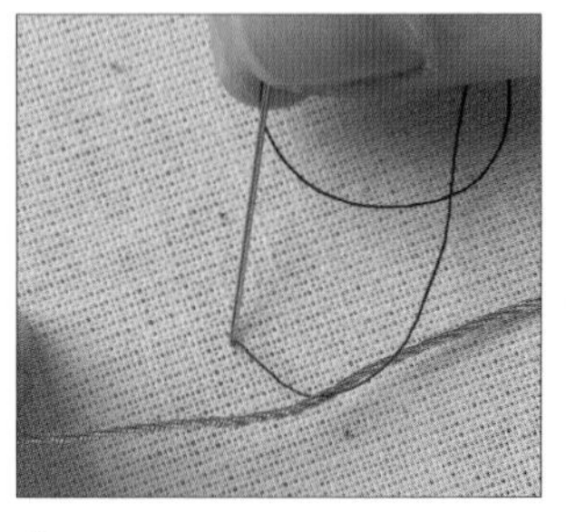

2 Take the needle back down through the same hole.

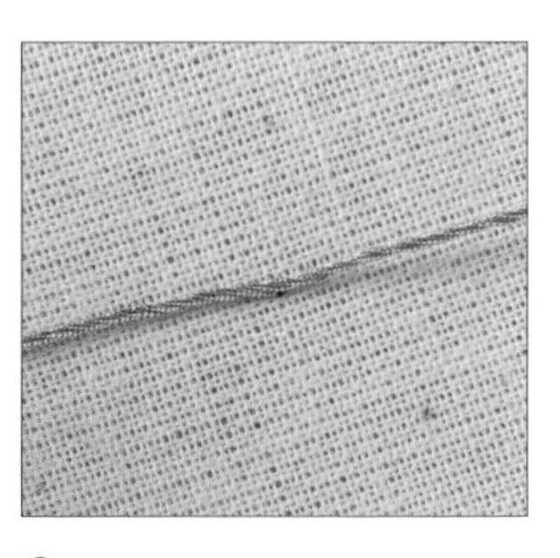

3 Pull the thread through to create an invisible stitch.

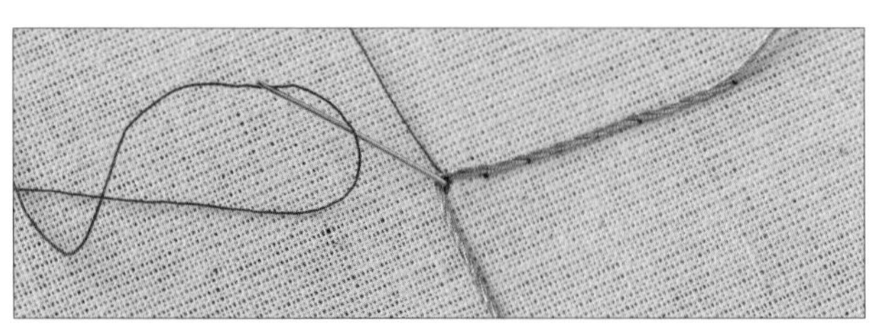

4 Continue stitching, passing the thread through the twist as described above and spacing the stitches approximately 3–4mm (¼in) apart. To turn a corner, bend the twist round at the last stitch made and place a second stitch over the top of it. Lay this stitch over all three strands to create a sharp corner. As you make the corner stitch, twist the end of the gold thread tightly in the direction of the plies to hold them together.

5 Continue stitching along the twist as before.

This pomegranate forms part of an early twentieth-century student-diploma piece using gold and cotton threads. Twist has been used to finish the edges of the fruit and leaves, and Elizabethan twist to embroider the leaves. The fleur de lys (page 56) and the crown (page 60) form the remainder of the piece. (RSN Collection)

BASKETWEAVE

Basketweave involves couching over hard string. This is a very versatile technique as you can lay the threads down in many different patterns. Begin by dyeing the hard string (generally using tea) to soften the colour (see page 40). When dry, run it gently through some beeswax to help make it a little more malleable, then cut it into several pieces, all the same length.

The fleur de lys which, along with the pomegranate on page 55 and the crown on page 60, forms part of an early twentieth-century student-diploma piece using gold and cotton threads. The fleur de lys features a basketweave pattern. (RSN Collection)

Applying the gold threads over the padding

There is a huge variety of basketweave patterns that can be achieved by stitching over different numbers of strings in various combinations. Smooth metal threads, for example Japanese gold or smooth passing (which is the thread used in the demonstration below), generally work better than textured threads, which can create a confusing finish.

Begin by cutting two pairs of gold threads, approximately 4cm (1½in) longer than the padding at each end. Attach the first pair, then use the second pair to measure the third pair against and so on. That way, you will avoid cutting any threads the wrong length.

Note

For clarity, I have used a contrasting sewing thread in the demonstration, but it is best to use a self-coloured (matching) thread to work the hard-string padding.

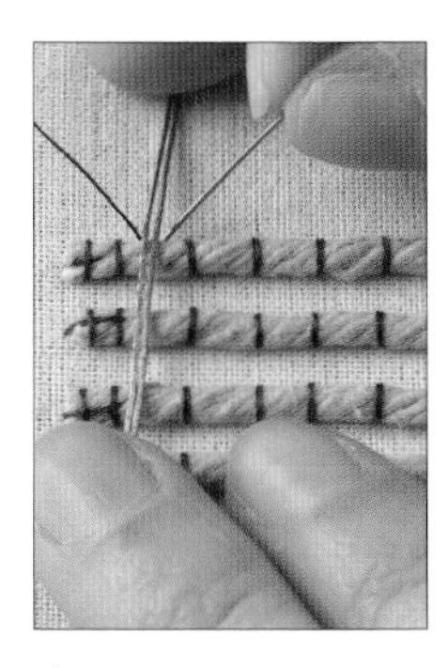

1 Lay a pair of gold threads across the padding and take a stitch over the gold using a suitable sewing thread, next to the top of the first string. Start a little way in from one side, as shown.

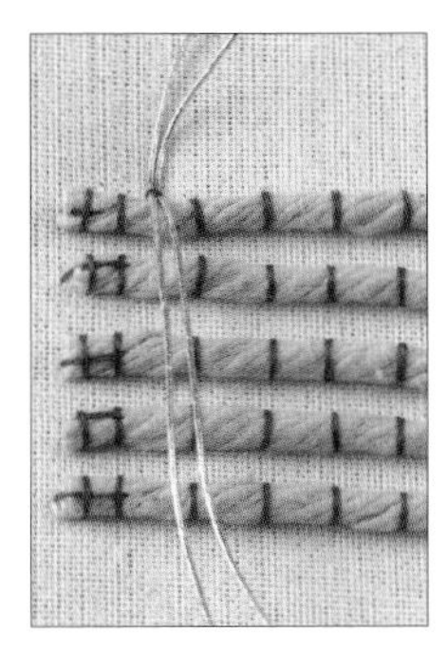

2 Pull the thread tightly so that it holds the gold firmly against the string.

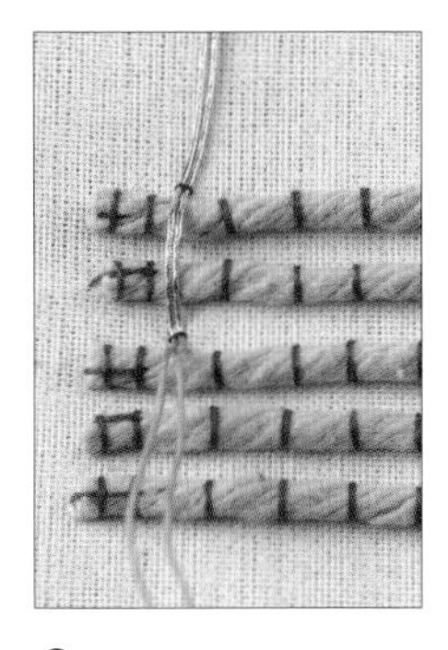

3 Take the gold threads over two strings and lay another stitch halfway between the second and third strings. Pull the stitch tight.

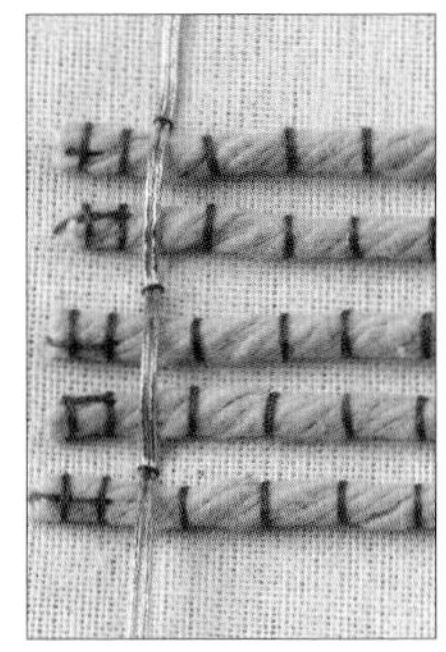

4 Lay the gold threads over each subsequent pair of strings, holding them in place with a stitch, as above. Keep the line of gold threads as straight as possible, and make sure it doesn't twist.

Note

Placing the first row of gold may initially displace the strings. After you have worked several more rows, the strings should look even again.

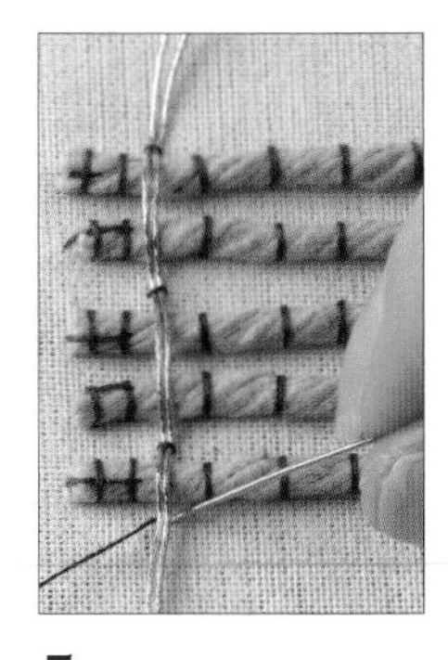

5 Finish the row with a small holding stitch over the gold threads, just below the last piece of string. Leave the thread in the needle and use it to work the next stitch.

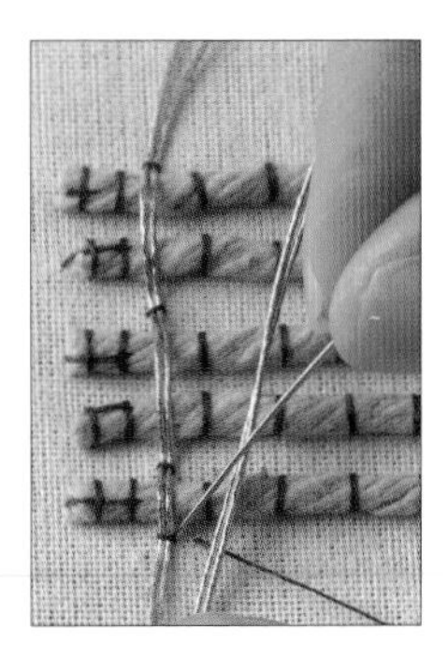

6 Lay the next pair of gold threads adjacent to the first. Work the first stitch over the threads next to the bottom of the last string.

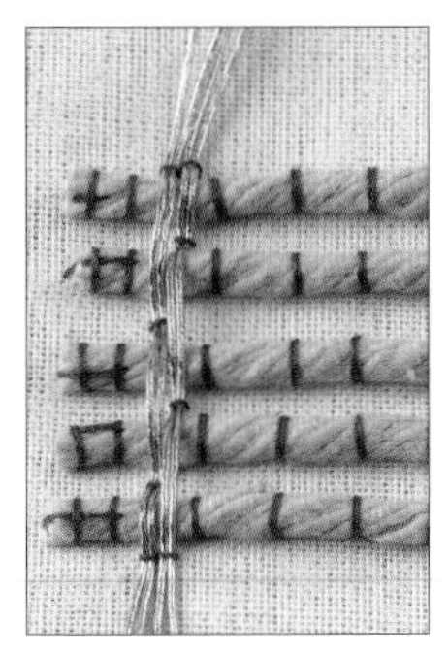

7 Work up towards the top of the padding, laying the gold over pairs of strings and finally over a single string. Work all the stitches from the outer edge inwards to help keep the lines of metal thread together.

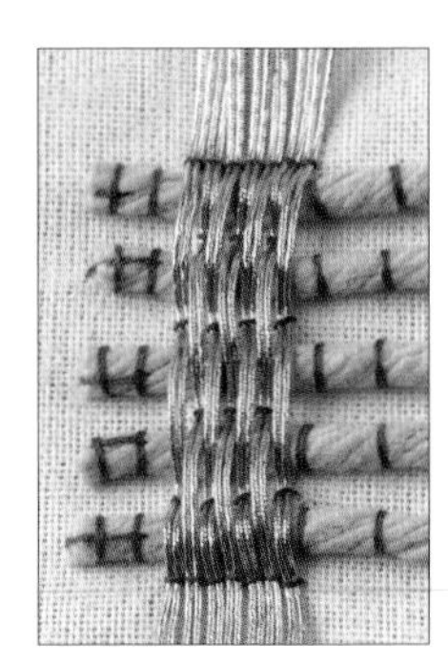

8 Continue in this way and gradually build up the basketweave pattern. Work up and down the rows of string, and across a little way to the right then out to the left.

Cutwork

Cutwork involves the cutting of soft-spiral or spring-like threads which have a hole in the middle. These need to be snipped down to the required size and then stitched down like a bead with a double thread through the central hole. These metals will need careful handling so that there are no sharp ends on the metal to catch on fibres and pull out. They also crush and crack easily. You can tell if a thread is cracked when a dark line appears across the surface of the metal. If this happens, you need to dispose of that thread or save it for creative metal thread embroidery, where it may come in useful. The threads often tarnish quicker from the cracks and this is a good reason to dispose of cracked threads for traditional metal thread work.

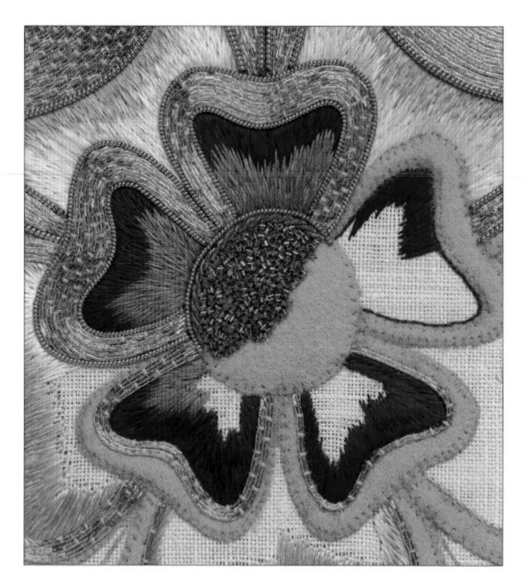

The centre of the Tudor Rose (see page 41) has been worked traditionally using small, flat chips, which give a dense, glittering finish.

Cutting the metal thread

We tend to use a gold board on which to cut the metal thread so that the threads are cushioned a little by the velvet's pile and are therefore protected from crushing. Also, the metal threads don't bounce around and get lost during the cutting process or once they are cut.

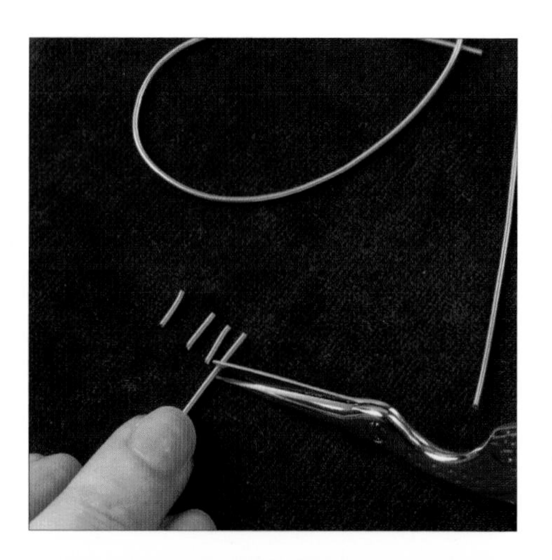

Cutting smooth purl into a number of small pieces, all the same length, on a gold board.

Note

Always keep a separate pair of scissors for cutting metal threads, as this can damage the blades.

CUTWORK CHIPS OVER FELT

There are clearly many different colours of metal thread that can be used to execute cutwork, but generally bright or dull check are used to fill areas with chips. These can be purchased in differing scales, which creates a variety of different effects.

> *Note*
>
> *Always use a double sewing thread when going through a metal thread, and a single sewing thread when couching over a metal thread.*

Copper and gold bright check, randomly placed at different angles to create a glittering, metallic surface. The chips have been cut relatively long in order to provide a looped, rough textural finish.

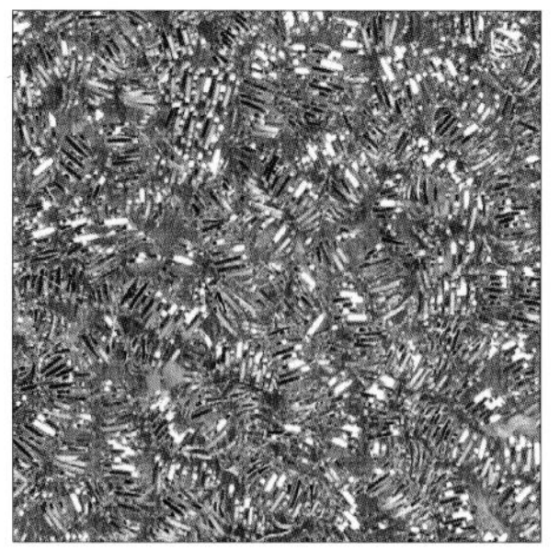

Traditionally, the chips are cut slightly shorter than those shown here, which results in them overlapping slightly and creating a texural finish.

Attaching the cutwork chips

Chips are most commonly cut into very small pieces and stitched down flat, at random angles, to create a glittering surface of metal, as in the Tudor Rose opposite. They can also be cut longer and stitched down into loops or so that they overlap each other to create entirely different textures and effects. The following demonstration shows how to attach cutwork chips.

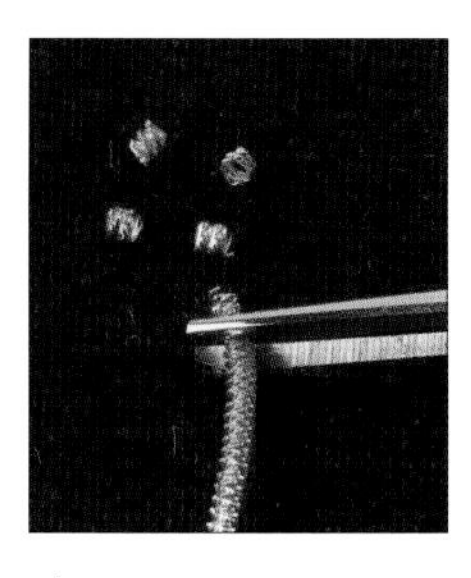

1 Cut tiny pieces from a length of gold thread and retain them on a gold board.

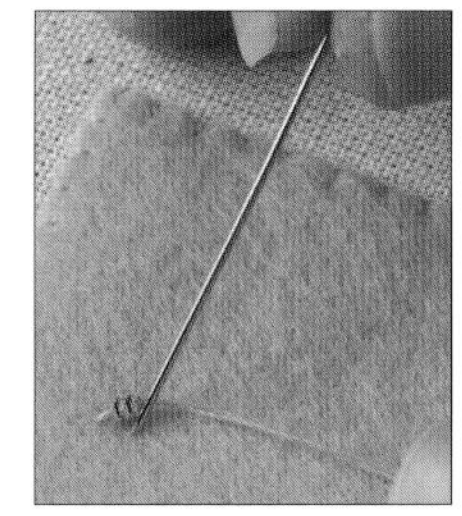

2 Bring a waxed, doubled thread through to the front and pick up a chip with the needle. Push the chip down to the end of the thread and secure it with a tiny stitch.

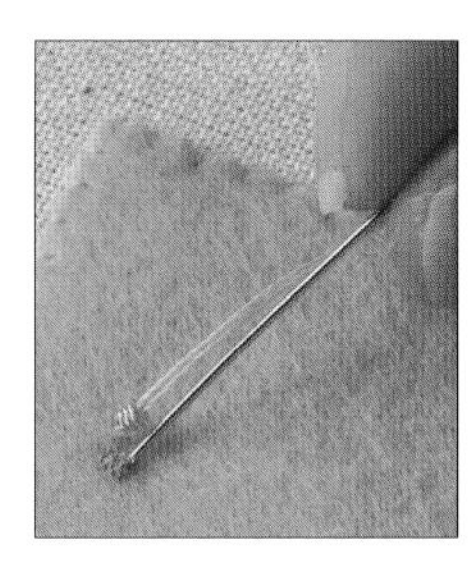

3 Position a second chip next to the first, varying the angle, and secure it in the same way.

4 Continue to add chips until the desired effect is achieved. The chips should be worked to fill the whole shape densely, as desired, so that none of the felt is visible. Smaller chips can be added at the end to fill any little gaps.

> *Note*
>
> *For a smooth finish, make sure the stitch you use to attach each chip is long enough for the chips to lie flat. For a more textured finish, shorten the stitch to force the chips into a curve and overlap them slightly.*

The crown which, along with the pomegranate on page 55 and the fleur de lys on page 56, forms part of an early twentieth-century student-diploma piece using gold and cotton threads. Cutwork is shown in the form of chips applied to the top, decorative section of the crown; cutwork over soft string has been utilised in the two narrow horizontal bands bordering the lower section; and s-ing has been worked around the jewels. (RSN Collection)

CUTWORK PURLS OVER FELT

Cutwork is mostly seen over high padding to give a sculptural feel to a piece, but it can be worked flat to the ground fabric or over craft-felt padding as well as over soft-string padding. The finished result looks very different depending on the pattern, angle and types of threads used, as well as the level of padding.

1 Thread a needle with a double thread and wax it. Start the thread (see page 34) a purl's length from the edge of the shape and pick up a single purl on the end of the needle. Avoid touching the gold.

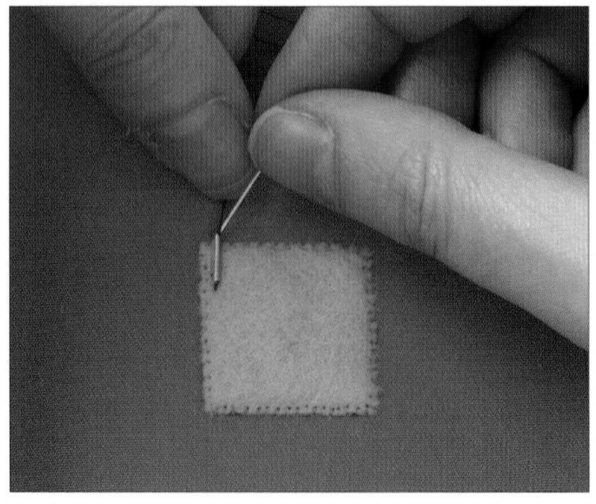

2 Take the purl down to the end of the thread and nudge it right to the end using the needle.

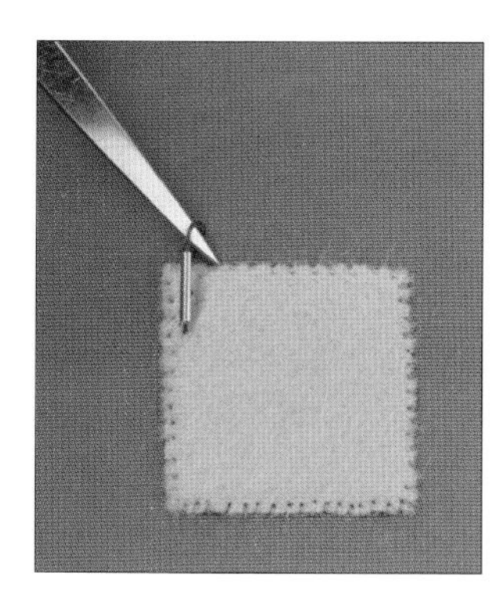

3 Take the thread down at the edge of the felt. Use the point of a mellor to make sure the thread runs smoothly and prevent it from knotting.

4 Pull the thread tight to secure the purl and bring the needle back through adjacent to the end of the first stitch. Pick up another purl and position it next to the first. Make sure the two purls lie parallel, with no gap in between.

5 Continue to lay the purls in parallel lines.

6 To create a chequerboard pattern, attach enough purls to make a square, then change to a different coloured smooth purl and lay the cut purls at 90° to those in the first row.

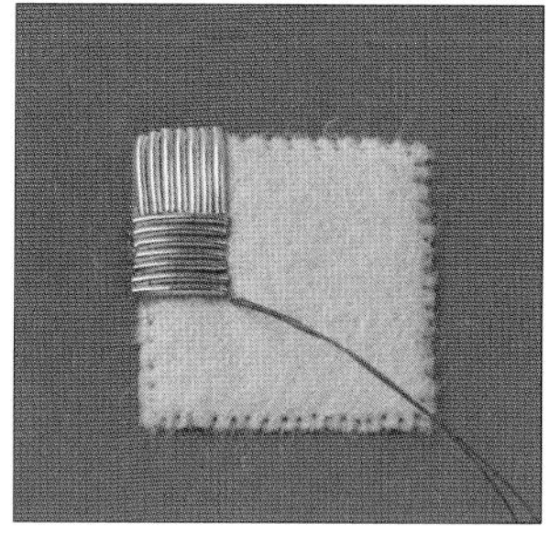

7 Complete the second row of purls.

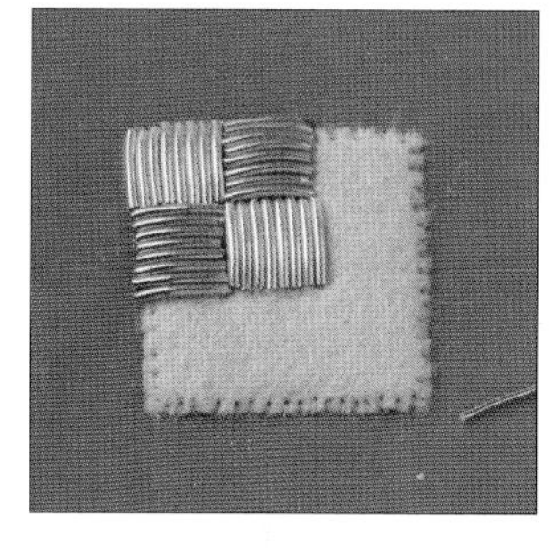

8 Build up the chequerboard pattern, using alternately gold and copper-coloured purls.

Note

A contrasting sewing thread has been used here for clarity, but in reality a self-coloured thread would be used.

CUTWORK PURLS OVER SOFT STRING

As previously illustrated, cutwork may be worked flat to the fabric or over craft felt, but it is most commonly used over soft-string padding to create a dramatic, sculptural effect. High-relief padding emphasises the textural qualities of the metal threads and also acts as a stable support.

***Still Waters Flow* (detail)**

Helen McCook

This enlarged section of a finished piece includes an example of cutwork over soft string, spangles, beads, pearl purl, overstretched pearl purl with a coloured core, twist, silver passing thread with coloured bricking, s-ing, kid and patterned couching. The entire piece is shown on page 78.

Attaching cutwork purls over soft string

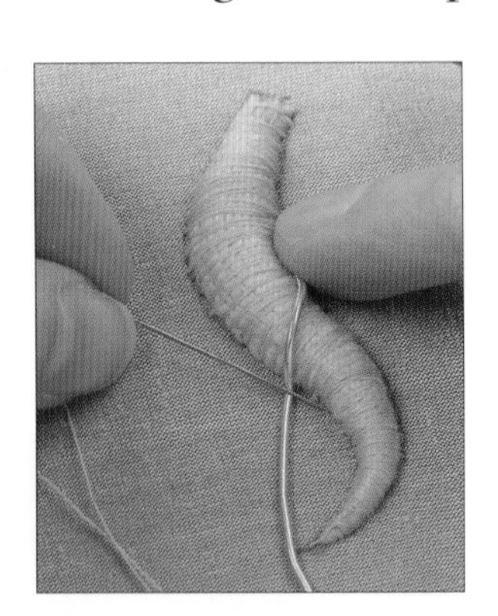

1 Using a waxed double thread, bring the needle up from underneath the padding approximately halfway along the right-hand side. The thread should be just touching the padding. Take a length of stretched pearl purl. Starting where the sewing thread comes through the fabric, take the gold across the padding at 45° so that it hugs the padding. Hold it firmly in place and use the needle to dent the gold at the point where it meets the fabric. This dent marks the length to which you need to cut the purls.

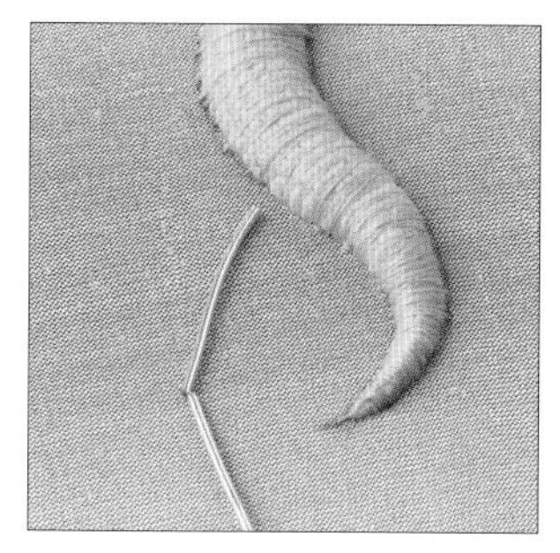

The dented smooth purl, marking the length of the cut purls.

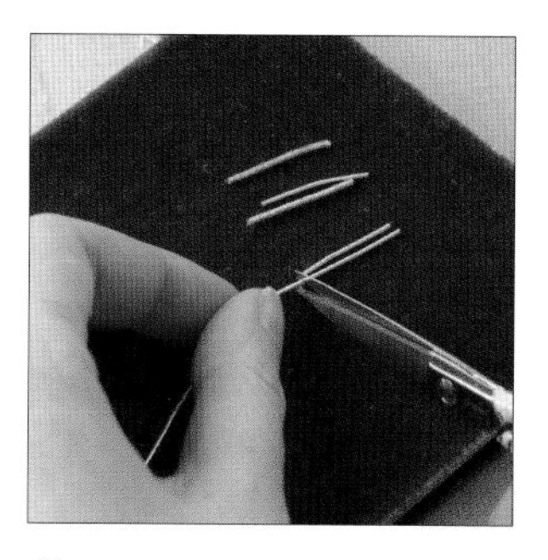

2 Working on a gold board, cut off the first purl at the dent using a pair of very sharp scissors and use it as a guide for cutting off several more.

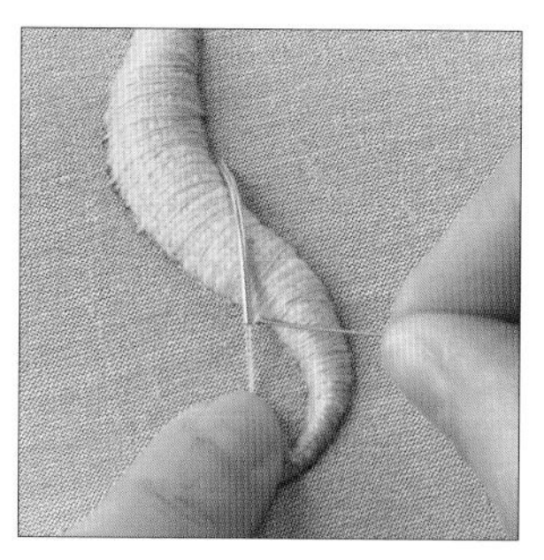

3 Working with the cut purls nearby, pick up a purl with the needle and take it gently down to the base of the thread. Lay it across the padding at a 45° angle. Take the needle down through the fabric, close to the side of the padding and tucked underneath so that the gold hugs the padding.

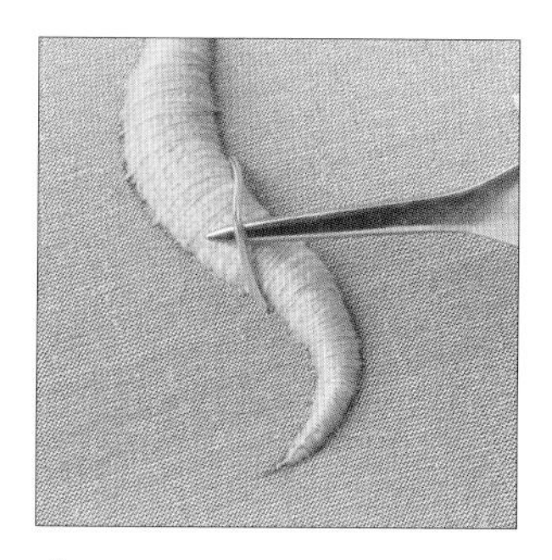

4 Place the tip of a mellor under the gold to ease it into shape and prevent it from cracking.

5 Bring the needle up a little below the first purl on the left-hand side, allowing enough room for the second purl to just touch the first. Pick up a second purl and attach it as before.

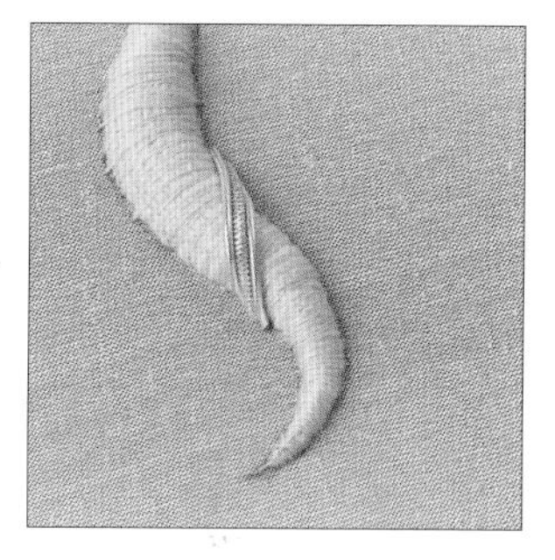

6 Attach the rest of the purls, working first towards the bottom of the padding and then towards the top. Here I have alternated smooth and bright check to enhance the pattern.

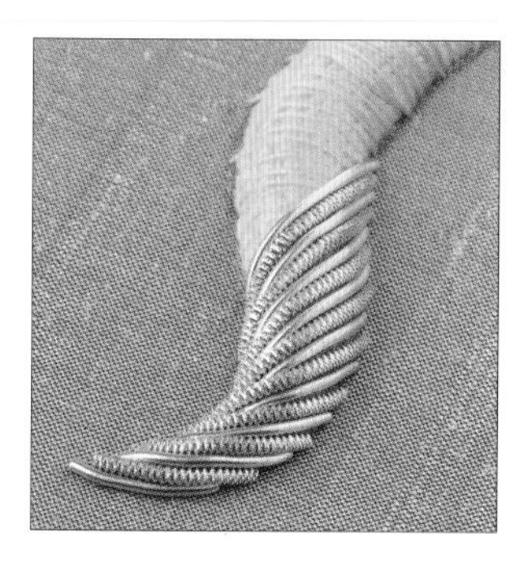

The partly worked cutwork over padding.

Note

Allow slightly more room for the gold where the needle comes up than where it goes down, as the second purl will naturally roll towards the first as the thread is tightened.

FLAT CUTWORK

Cutwork can also be worked flat on to the face of the base fabric or over a single layer of felt. The following demonstration illustrates this.

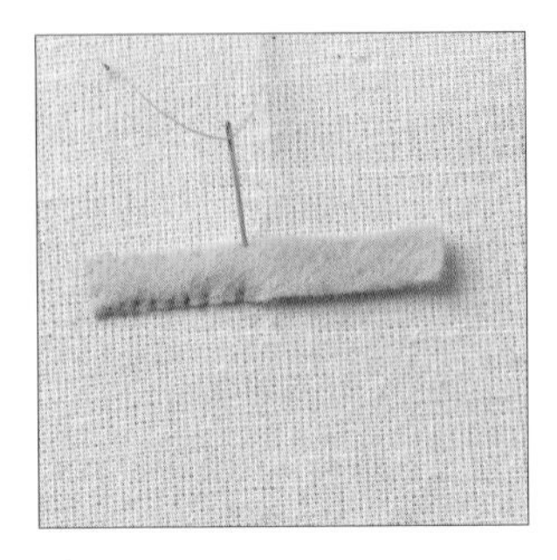

1 Cut a single strip of felt and attach it to the background fabric using tiny stab stitches worked 2–3mm (about ⅛in) apart (see the section on felt padding, page 42).

2 Begin with a waxed double thread and bring the needle through to the front of the fabric from underneath the felt, close to the bottom edge of the shape. Hold the length of smooth purl across the shape and dent it using the needle at the point where it touches the fabric on the other side. Snip off the purl at this point and use it as a guide to measure and cut several more. Pick up a purl with the needle and push it gently to the end of the thread. Stitch the purl in place, working at right angles to the felt.

3 Work the subsequent purls in the same way. Working over a single layer of felt produces a pleasing curve that complements the gold well.

Note

Cut purls can be attached at either 90° or 45° to the felt, depending on the effect you wish to achieve. When working at 90°, you can start to attach the purls at one end and work along to the other. When working at 45°, it is better to start in the middle of the shape and work first to one end and then to the other.

Kid

The application of kid is a good way to cover an area swiftly or to create a smooth effect. It is available in various colours and textures and, as mentioned previously, faux kid leather is available. Kid can be attached directly to the background fabric, or worked over felt or soft-string padding. The method is the same in each case. If you are applying a large piece of kid, you may wish to baste it to the fabric prior to stitching to hold it in place.

Note

If you are working an edging, always attach the kid before applying the edging. The demonstration shown here uses a coloured thread that is clearly visible against the kid, however if a self-coloured thread is used, the stitches will be virtually invisible.

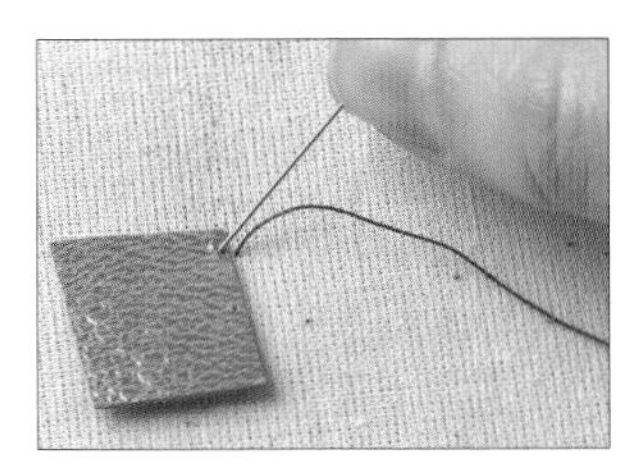

1 Using a single thread, bring the needle up through the fabric at the edge of the kid and take it down through the kid to form a tiny stitch.

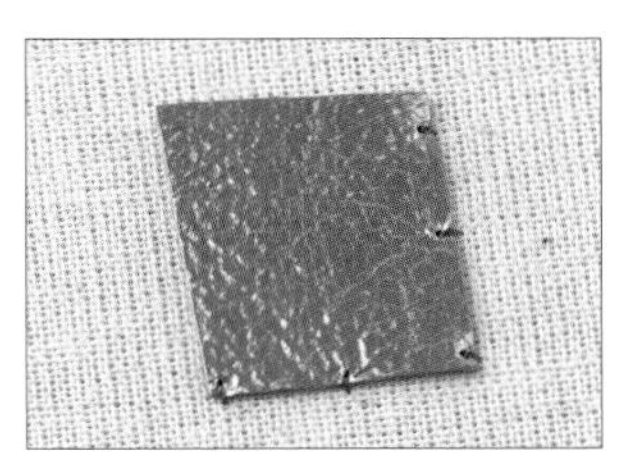

2 Begin by securing the kid using widely spaced stitches placed close to the corners and in the centre of each edge.

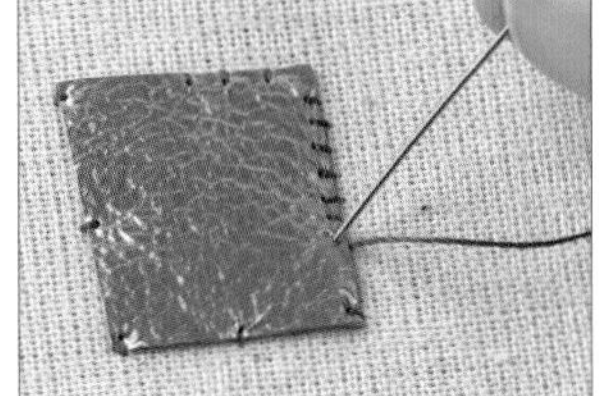

3 Work the stitches in between the initial holding stitches, spacing them approximately 2–3mm (about ⅛in) apart.

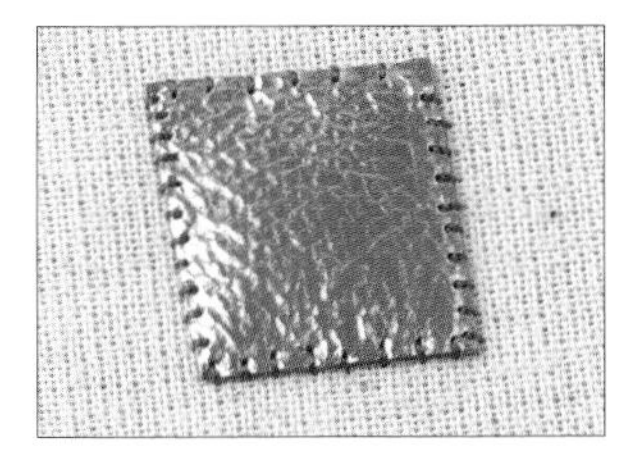

The kid stitched in place.

Note

Kid is a tough material to stitch through. Once you have inserted the needle into the kid, 'wiggle' it slightly to help ease it through. Wear a thimble to protect your fingers. You may wish to consider using a leather needle when applying kid as it will cut through the kid easier than a normal embroidery needle. Do be aware that they are very sharp, however.

Transferring a shape to kid

1 Lay the template face down on the back of the kid and draw round it using a fine-liner pen.

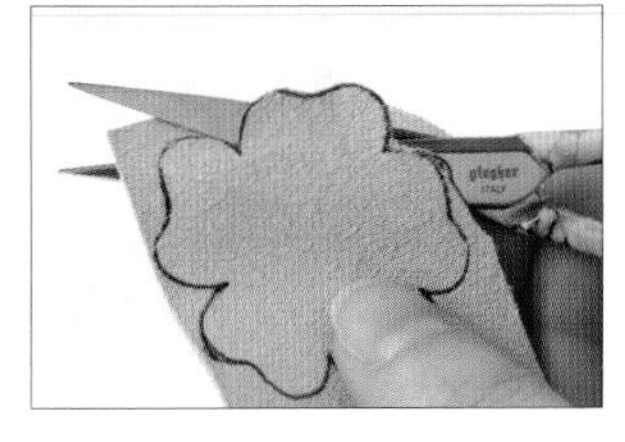

2 Snip around the shape.

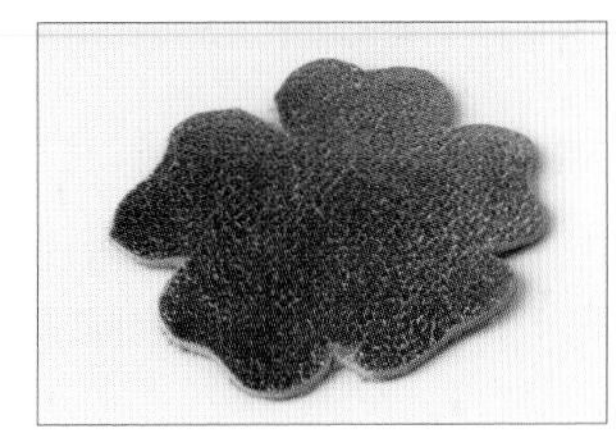

The cut-out shape.

S-ING

S-ing is essentially stem stitch worked in metal threads. It can be used to create a fine, sinuous line of metal with a rope-like appearance or it can be executed using longer pieces of metal which may be stitched to create interlinking loops when viewed from the side. S-ing may also be used with spangles.

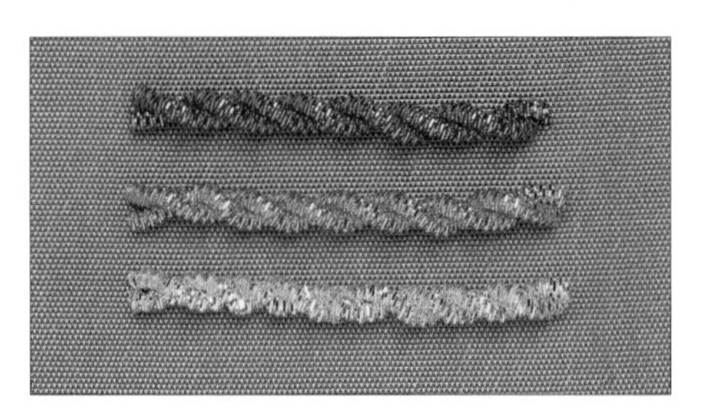

S-ing with copper, gold and silver bright check purl.

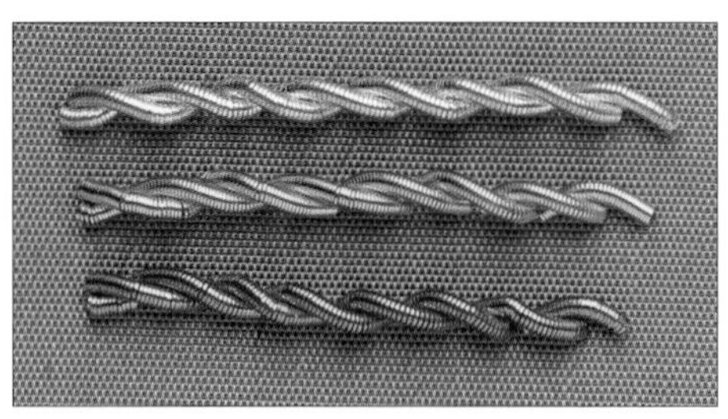

S-ing with copper, gold and silver smooth purl.

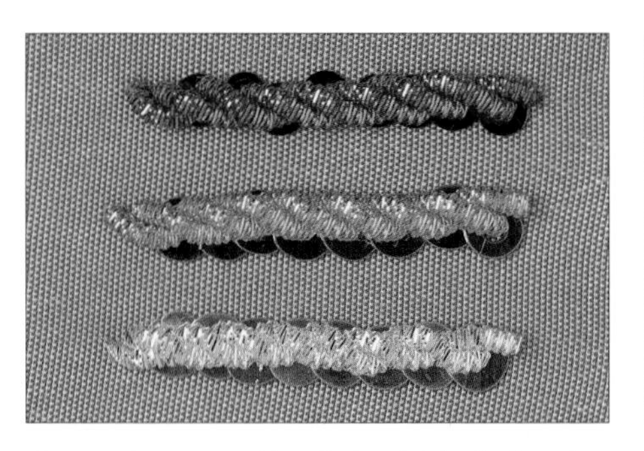

S-ing with copper, gold and silver bright check purl with spangles.

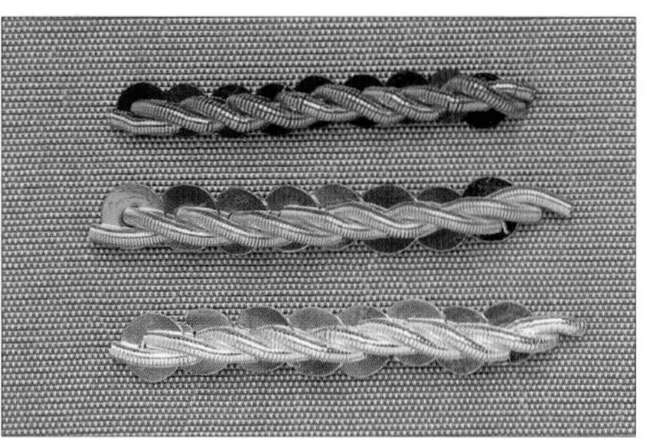

S-ing with copper, gold and silver smooth purl and spangles.

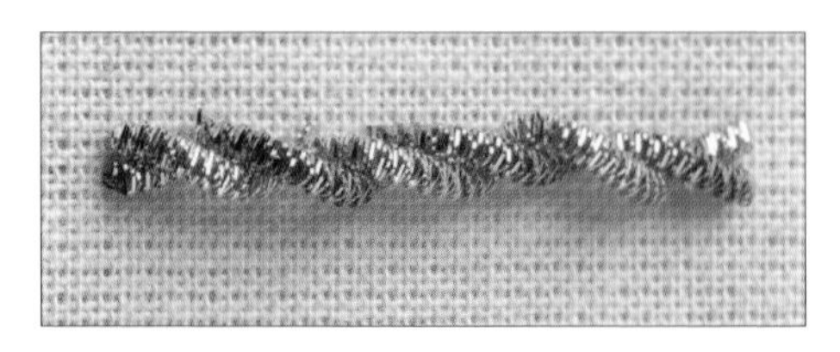

Looped s-ing with gold and copper bright check.

Looped s-ing with spangles and smooth purl.

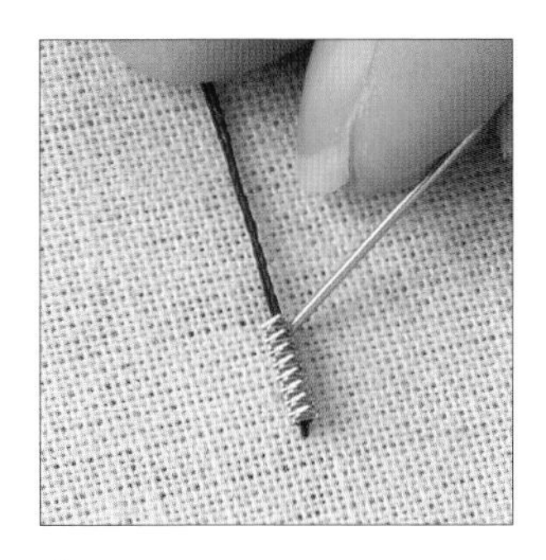

1 Cut several equal short lengths of gold and copper purl on a gold board. Take a waxed double thread and bring the needle through to the front of the fabric. Pick up a gold purl with the needle and push it down to the end of the thread. Lay it flat, and take the needle back down just underneath the end of the purl.

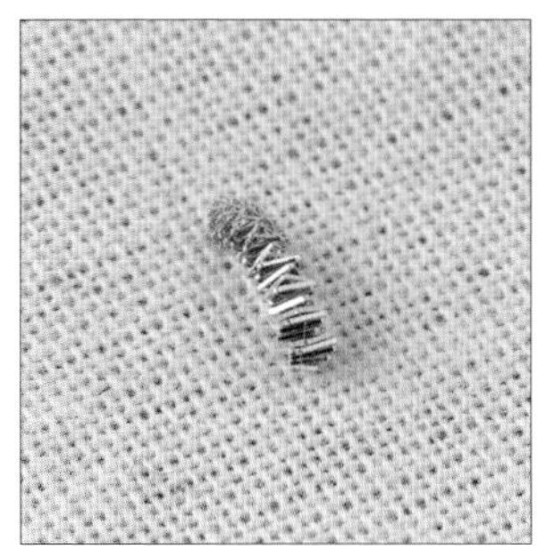

2 Pull the thread through so that the purl lies flat against the surface of the fabric.

3 Bring the needle and thread back through about half-a-purl's length in front of the purl.

Note

Take care when s-ing not to damage your previous purl with your needle or by pulling the thread too tight.

4 Pick up a copper purl and push it to the end of the thread. Take the needle down under the first purl and approximately halfway along.

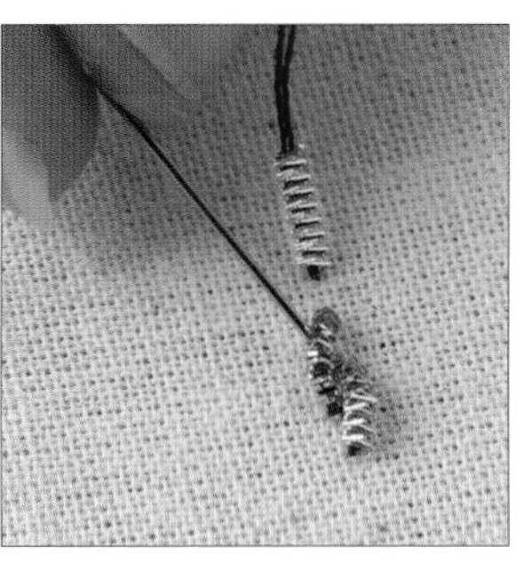

5 Secure the purl, then bring the needle through about half-a-pearl's length in front of it, as in step 3, and thread on a gold purl.

The first three purls.

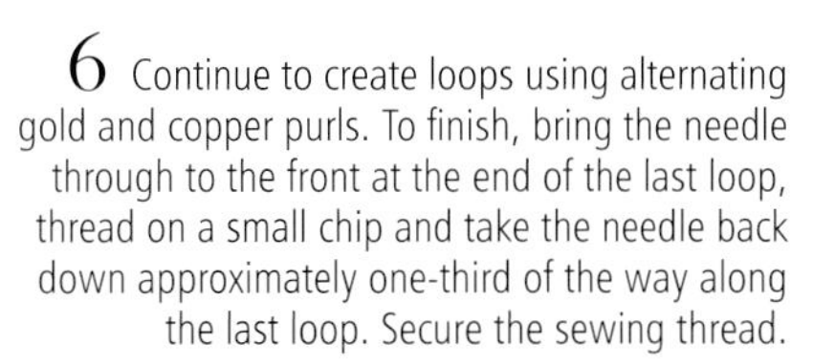

6 Continue to create loops using alternating gold and copper purls. To finish, bring the needle through to the front at the end of the last loop, thread on a small chip and take the needle back down approximately one-third of the way along the last loop. Secure the sewing thread.

SPANGLES

Spangles may be stitched down in a variety of decorative ways, either individually or in lines. You may decide that you want fancy stitching with coloured silk threads. Alternatively, they could be held down with chips, looped chips, beads or, invisibly, in fish-scale-style stitching which results in the overlapping spangles concealing the stitch which holds down the previous spangle.

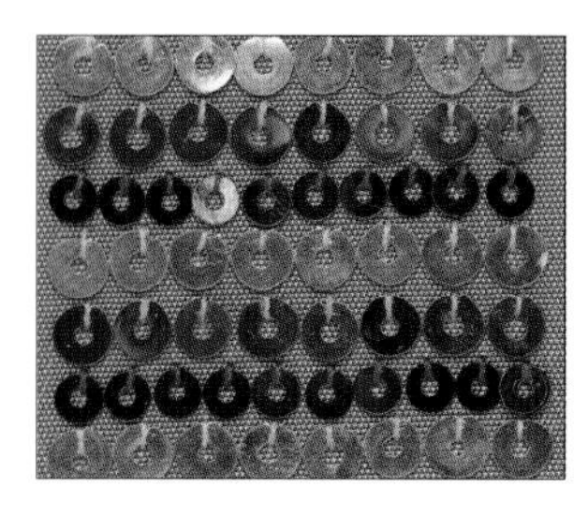

3mm copper sequins and 4mm gold and silver spangles worked in rows. Each spangle is held down with a single stitch.

Spangles worked in a random pattern, each held down with a chip.

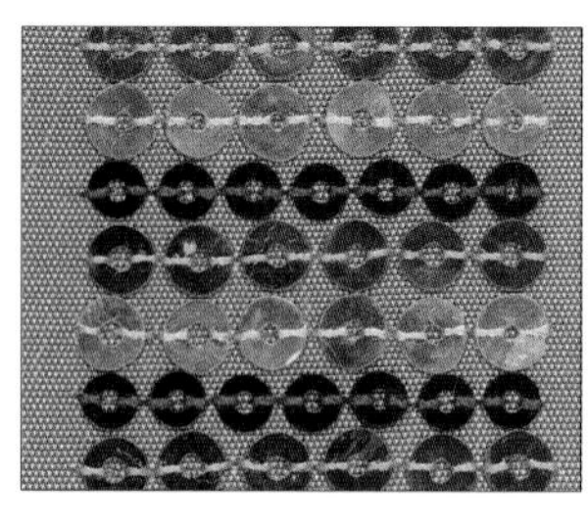

Rows of spangles, each held down with two stitches.

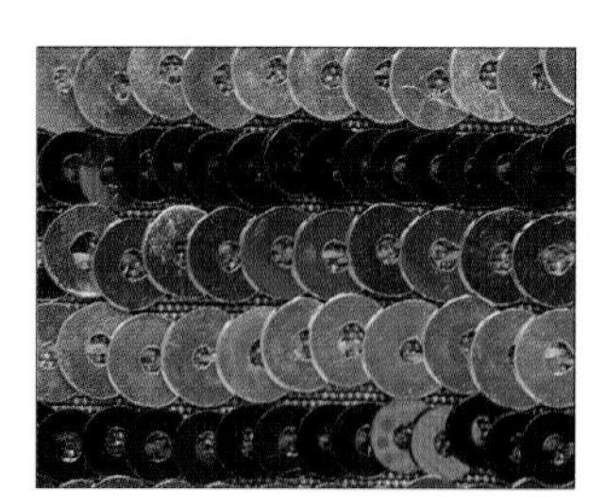

Spangles worked in a fish-scale design. The spangles are overlapped to hide the stitching.

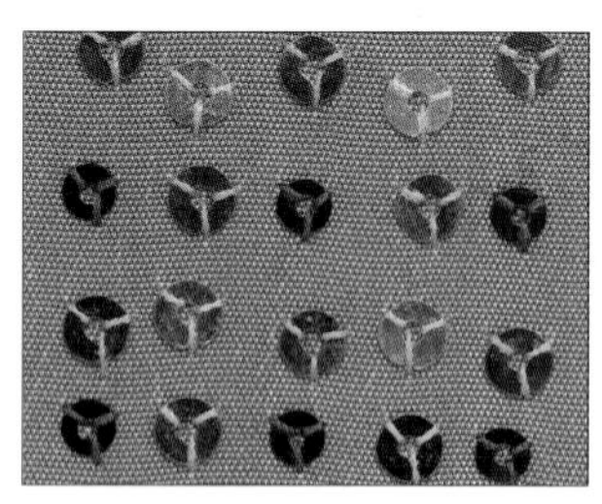

Spangles held down with three stitches.

Spangles held down with beads.

SPANGLES HELD ON WITH PURLS

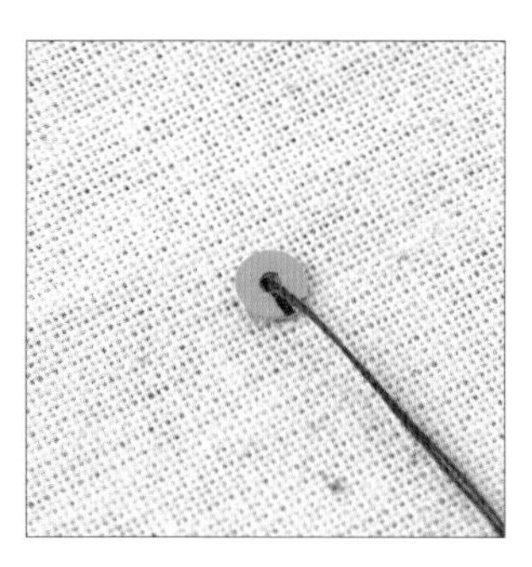

1 Take a waxed double thread and bring the needle through to the front of the fabric. Thread on a spangle and push it down to the end of the thread.

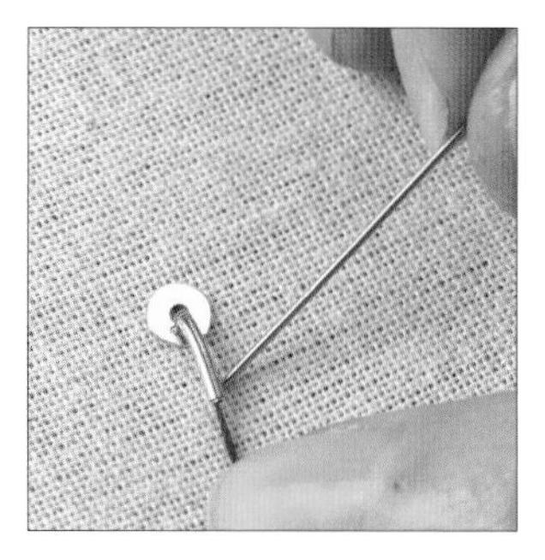

2 Pick up a purl with the needle and push it to the end of the thread. Lay the purl flat and take the needle down underneath it about one-third of the way back along its length.

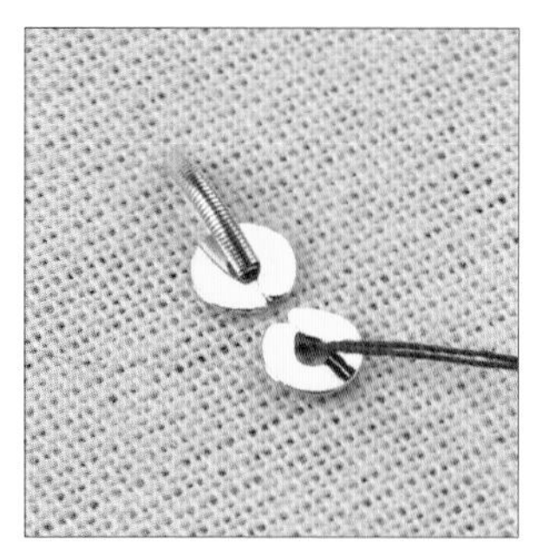

3 Pull the thread through and bring the needle out on the other side of the spangle. Make sure the ridge on the spangle is concealed underneath the purl. Thread on another spangle and push it down to the end of the thread.

4 Pick up another purl and push it to the end of the thread. Take the needle through to the back on the opposite edge of the first spangle. Use the pointed end of a mellor to guide and shape the purl carefully.

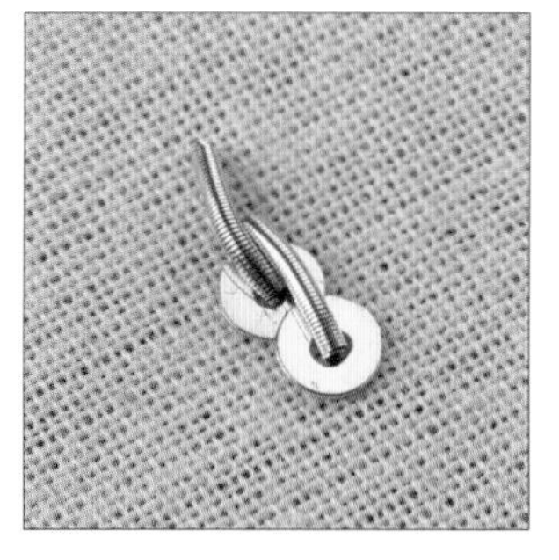

5 Pull the thread through to tighten the stitch.

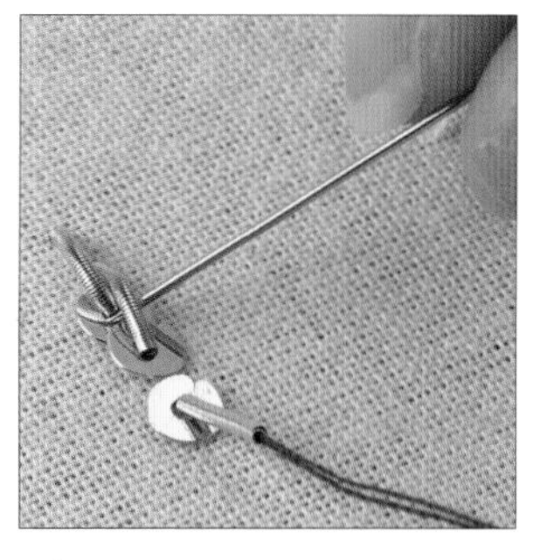

6 Bring the needle back through just above the second spangle and thread on a third spangle. Pick up a purl and this time take the needle down through the hole in the centre of the first spangle.

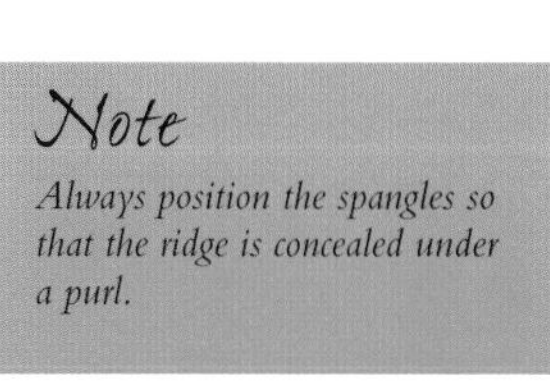

Note

Always position the spangles so that the ridge is concealed under a purl.

7 Continue in this pattern, taking the needle down through the second spangle back from the one you are securing. To finish, work a final purl without the addition of a spangle. Fasten off the thread on the back.

Plate

Plate is a thin, flat metal which can have a smooth or textured surface. It can be used flat or over hard or soft string, and may be stitched so that it is folded back on itself. Either no gaps can be left; gaps left unfilled; or gaps left and filled with decorative stitches, beads or chips of metal.

Whipped plate folded backwards and forwards across a shape with no gaps.

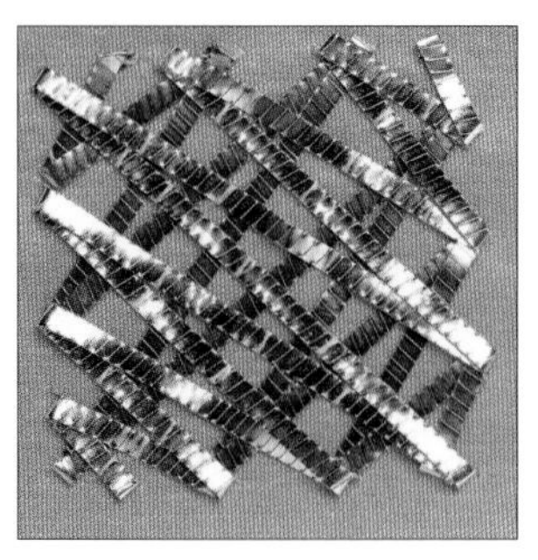

Whipped plate worked in an open pattern to create texture.

Whipped plate worked in an open grid pattern with spangles and chips in the gaps.

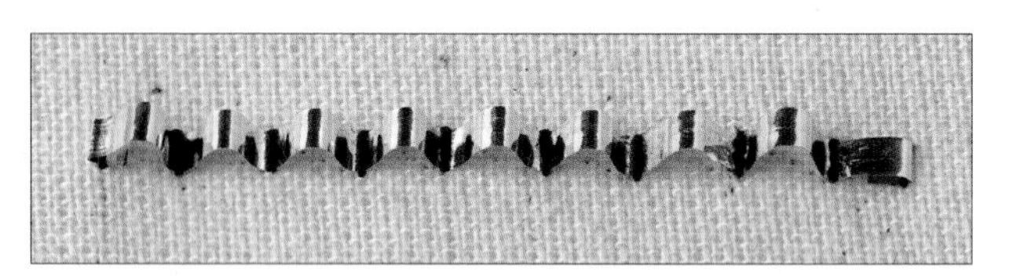

Crinkle plate attached with a coloured thread.

Crinkle plate attached with beads.

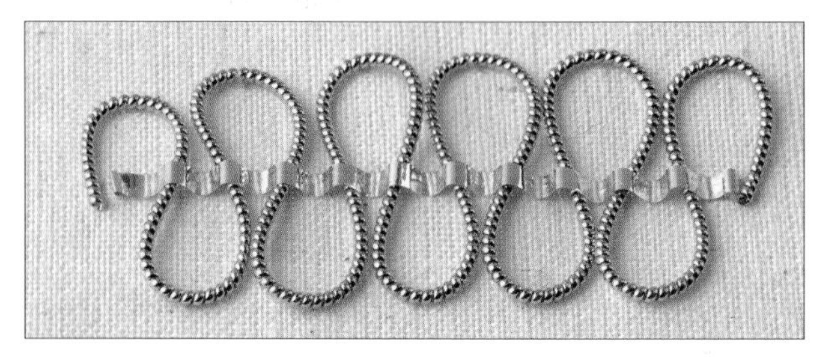

Crinkle plate with pearl purl.

ATTACHING PLATE OVER SOFT STRING

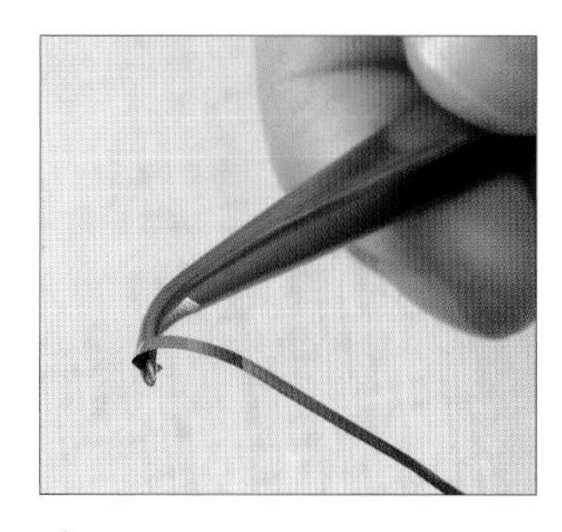

1 Begin by creating a hook at one end of the plate using a pair of curved tweezers.

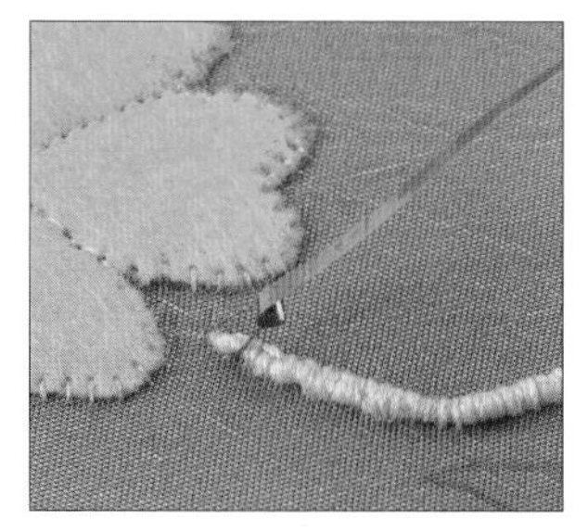

2 Make a loose stitch on the fabric, positioned where you wish to attach the end of the plate, and hook the end of the metal through the loop.

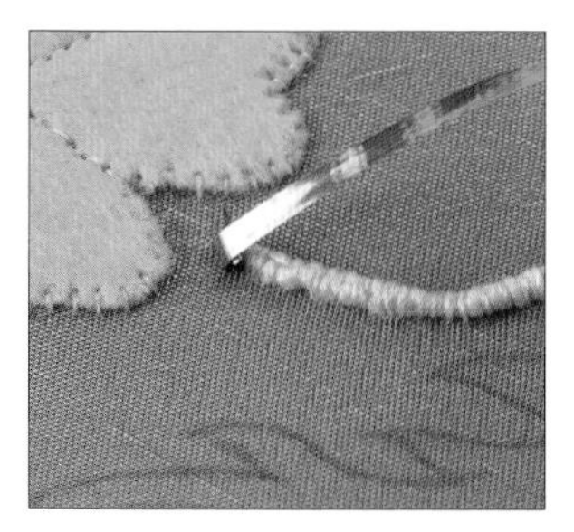

3 Pull the thread tight so that the plate lies securely against the fabric. Lay the metal across the padding, as shown.

Note

Use tweezers and a mellor to fold and position the plate rather than your fingers – handling the metal too much can cause it to tarnish.

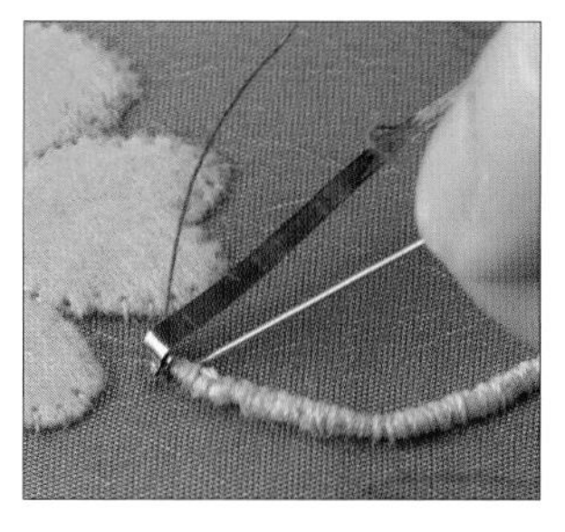

4 Place a second holding stitch over the plate, abutting the other side of the padding.

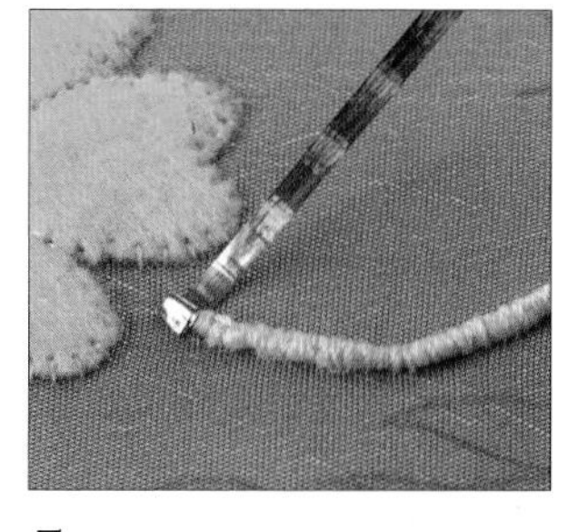

5 Pull the thread firmly to form a tight stitch.

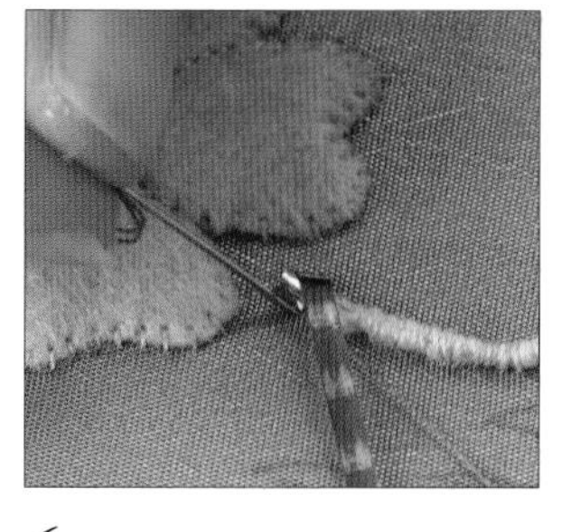

6 Fold the metal back across the padding at a slight angle, ensuring it covers more of the padding while at the same time overlapping the previously placed plate. Secure it with a holding stitch worked close to the padding, as in step 4.

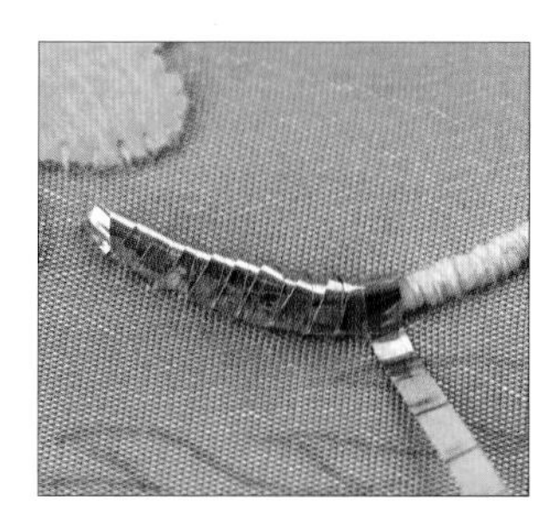

7 Continue working back and forth across the padding.

ATTACHING PLATE OVER FELT

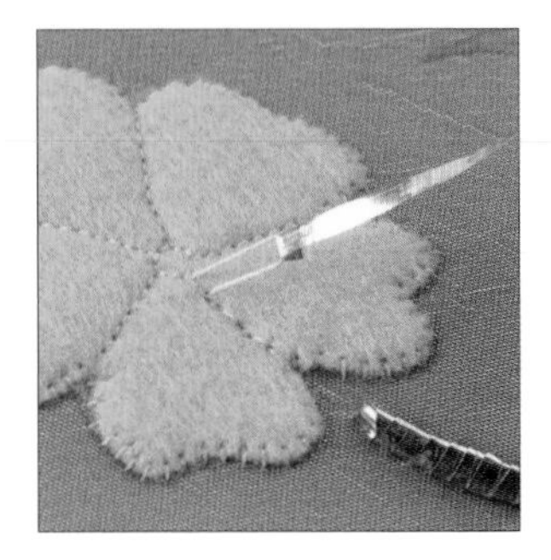

1 Begin by creating a hook at one end of the plate, as on page 71. Make a loose stitch on the felt where you wish to attach the end of the plate, and hook the end of the metal through the loop.

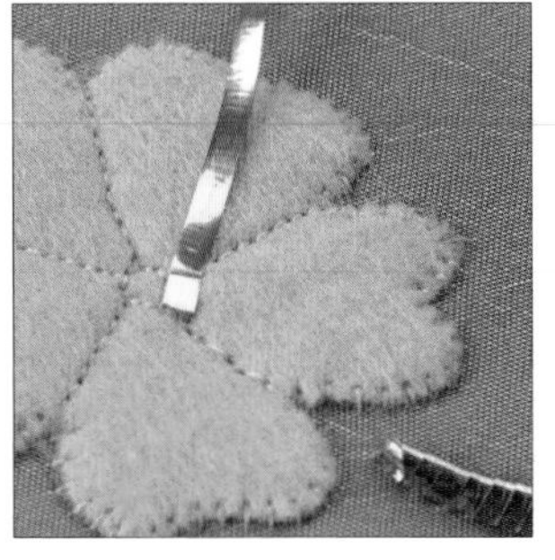

2 Pull the stitch tight to secure the metal to the felt. Lay the plate across the padding and secure it on the other side with another tight stitch.

3 Fold the plate across to the other side of the padding, angling it so as to cover more of the padding and overlap the previous row of plate.

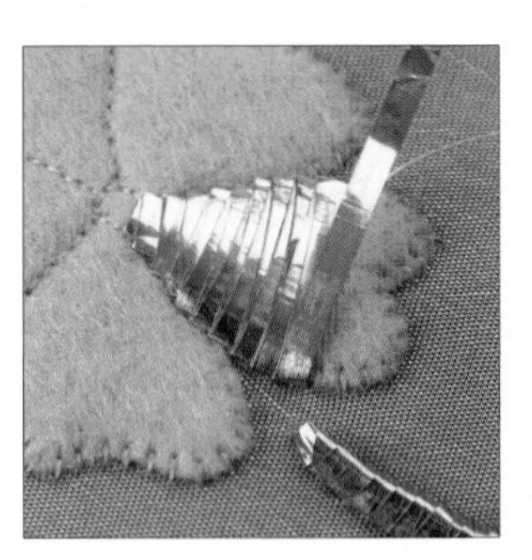

4 Place a stitch over the plate at the next fold, then bend the plate back in the opposite direction against the stitch, again at a slight angle. Continue in this way until the padded shape is covered.

5 Snip off the plate, leaving a sufficient length to bend under into a hook (as in step 1).

6 Secure the end of the metal with a stitch. Place two tiny stitches underneath the shape to secure it and finish the thread.

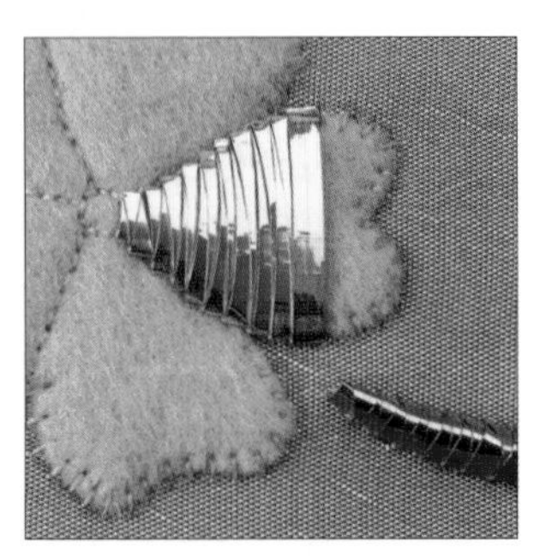

The completed plate over felt.

***Pomegranate and Gilly Flower** (detail)*
Helen McCook
Couched trellis with looped chips, overstretched pearl purl with coloured thread core, flat cutwork with beads and rough purl, feather stitch in rough purl, couching and surface stitching.

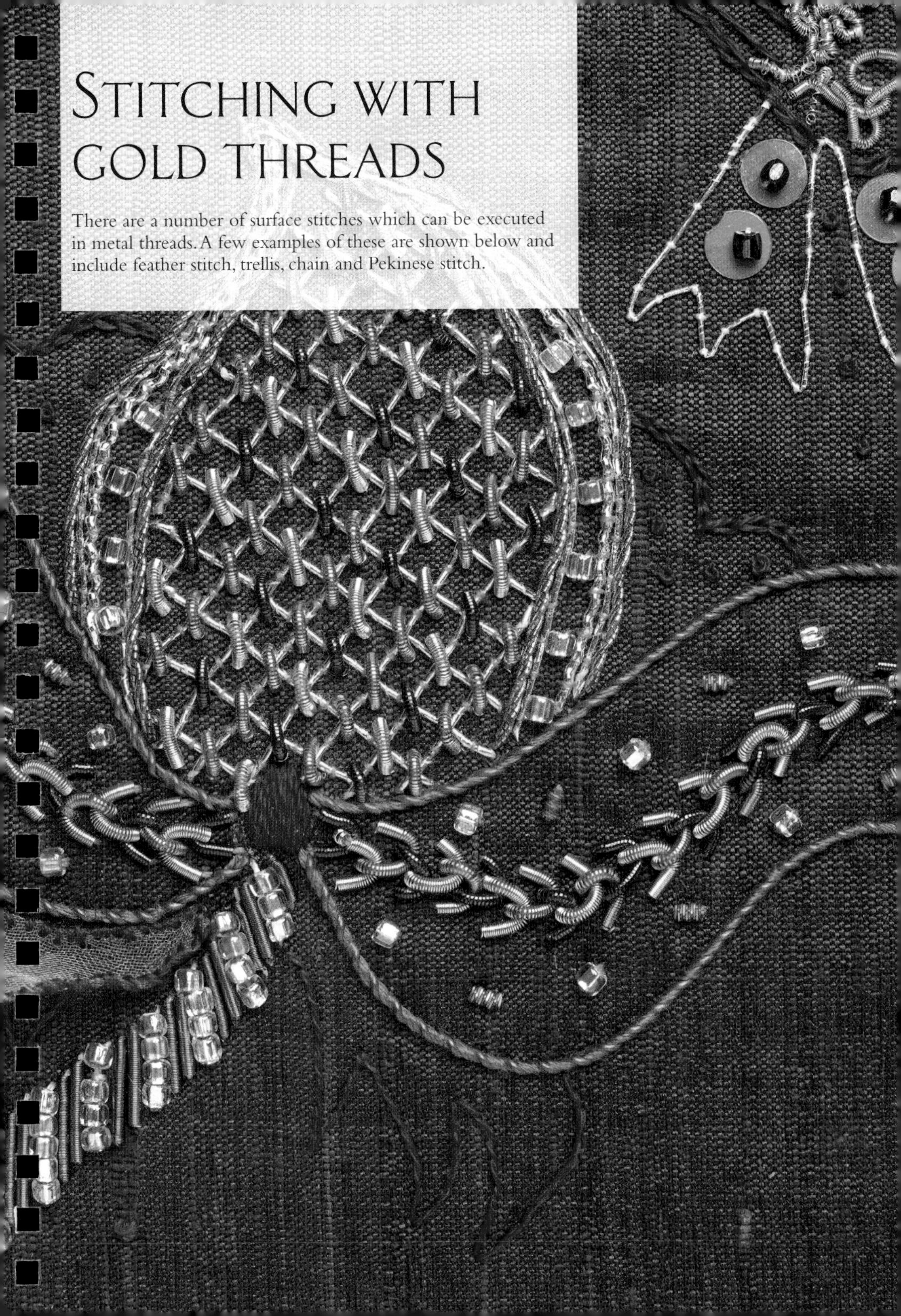

Stitching with gold threads

There are a number of surface stitches which can be executed in metal threads. A few examples of these are shown below and include feather stitch, trellis, chain and Pekinese stitch.

CHAIN STITCH

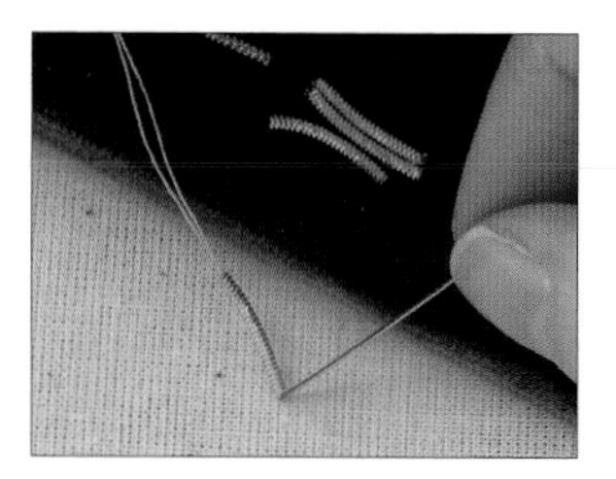

1 Take a waxed double thread and cut a number of short lengths of copper and gold bright check, all the same length. Bring the thread through to the front of the fabric and pick up a gold purl on the needle. Push the purl to the end of the thread and take the needle back down through the same hole.

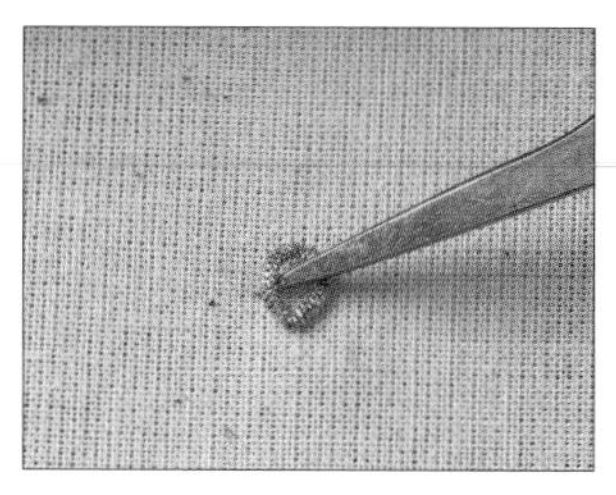

2 Pull the thread through and use the pointed end of a mellor to ease the metal into shape. This will help prevent twisting and cracking.

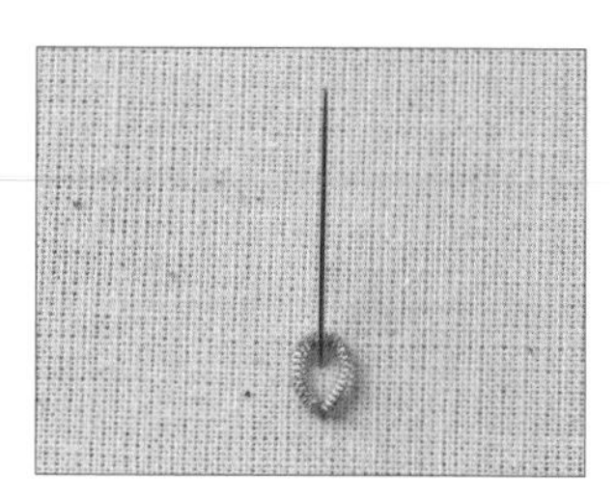

3 Bring the needle back through inside the loop.

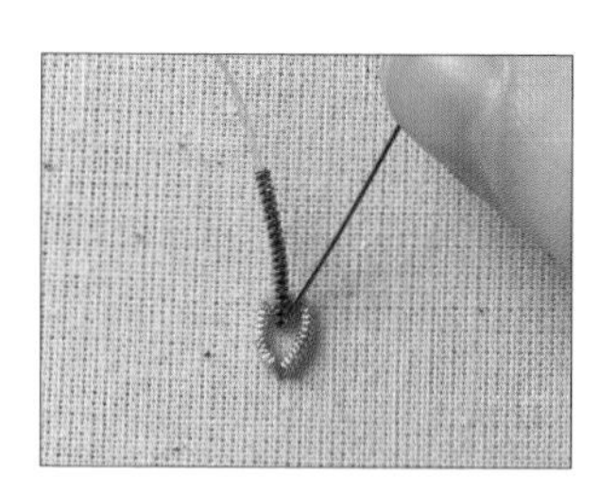

4 Pick up a copper purl and work a second stitch in the same way as before.

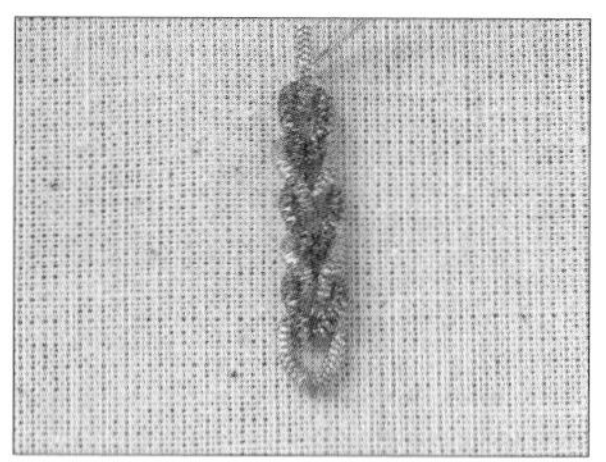

5 Continue to work stitches in alternate gold and copper purls, ensuring all the stitches are the same size. To finish, put a tiny purl in place at the end to hold the final stitch in place.

The completed chain stitch.

FEATHER STITCH

1 Take a waxed double thread and cut a number of short lengths of copper and gold bright check, all the same length. Bring the thread through to the front of the fabric and pick up a copper purl on the needle. Push the purl to the end of the thread and take the needle back down a stitch length to the right.

2 Guide the stitch around the pointed end of a mellor to ease it into a 'U' shape and to prevent the metal from twisting and cracking.

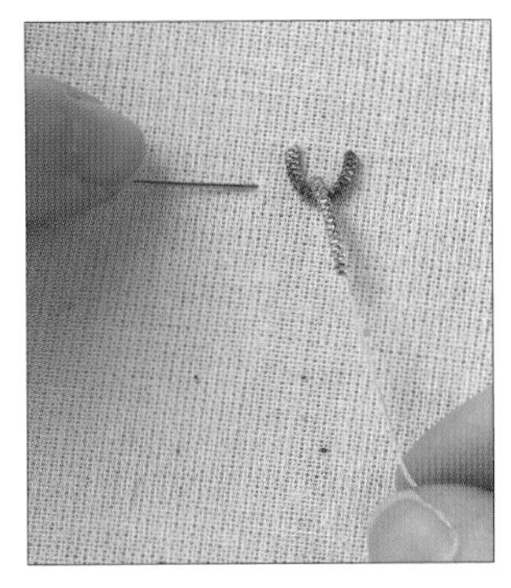

3 Bring the needle through to the front inside the loop, towards the base of the 'U', and pick up a gold purl on the needle. Push it down to the end of the thread and take the needle back down a little way to the left to create a second stitch. Make sure this stitch is the same size as the previous stitch.

4 Shape the stitch as before, using a mellor. Now bring the needle back through inside the loop. Pick up a copper purl and create the third stitch.

5 Continue to work stitches in alternate gold and copper purls, ensuring all the stitches are the same size. To finish, put a tiny purl in place at the end to hold the final stitch in place.

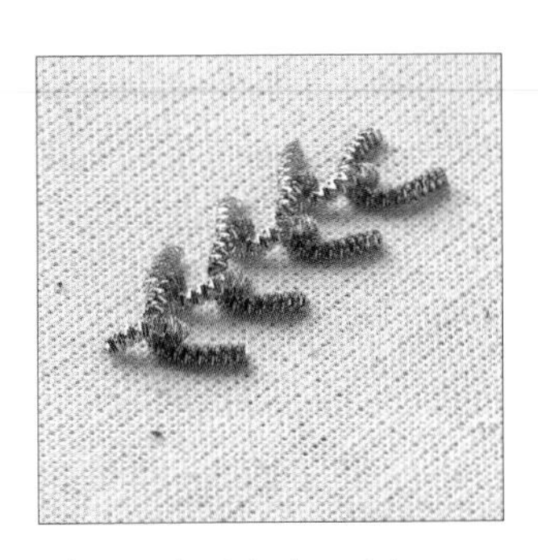

The completed feather stitch.

PEKINESE STITCH

1 Begin by working back stitch using six strands of six-stranded cotton. Keep the stitches as even as possible.

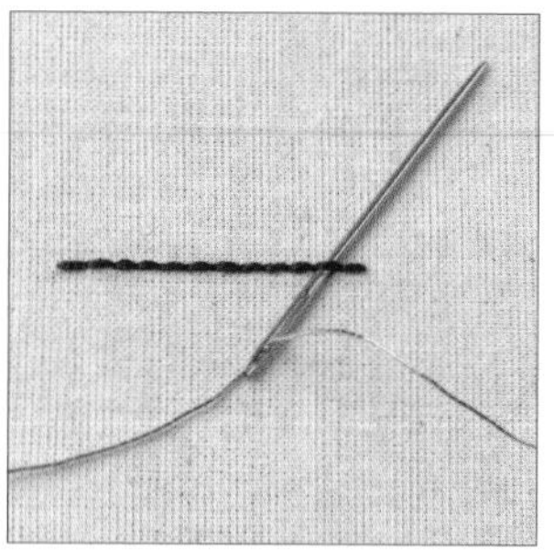

2 Thread a length of Japanese gold into a large needle (the hole should be large enough to accommodate the thread easily) and pass the needle underneath the second stitch from the right.

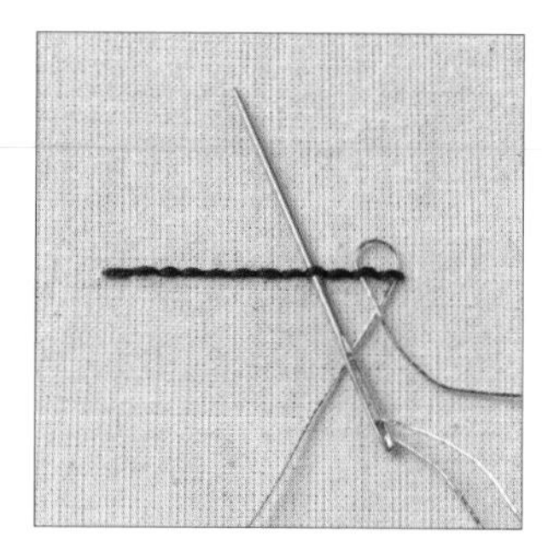

3 Take the thread underneath the first stitch in the opposite direction and pull it through to form a loop. Pass the needle underneath the fourth stitch in the same direction as it went through the second stitch.

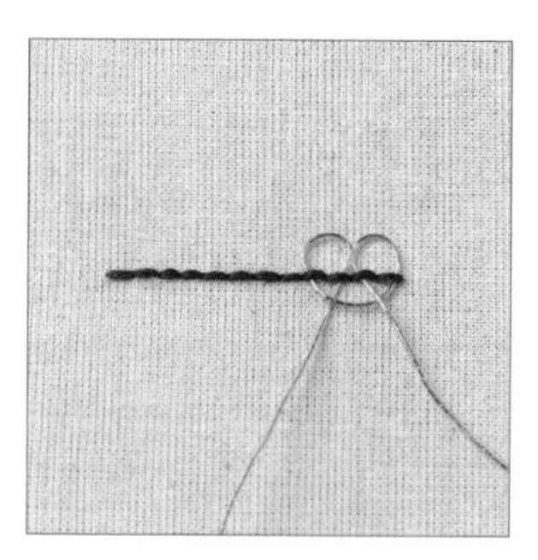

4 Pull the thread through to make a loop, then take the needle underneath the third stitch to form a second loop on the top of the line of back stitching. Try to make the loops as even as possible.

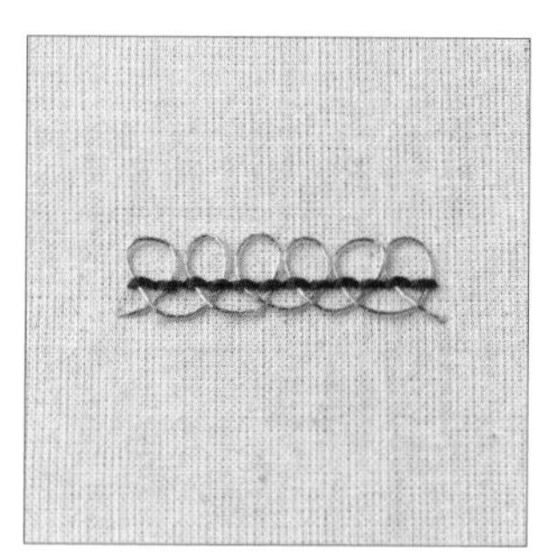

5 Continue in this pattern to form the Pekinese stitch. Finish by plunging and finishing the ends (see page 47).

Note

Be aware of the amount of tension on the gold thread while you are stitching – avoid pulling the thread too tight.

TRELLIS STITCH

1 Take a single strand of Japanese gold, lay it on the fabric and stitch over the gold near one end.

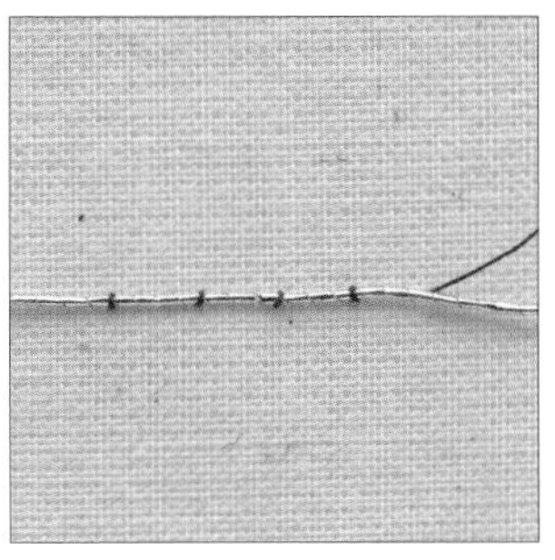

2 Continue stitching along the gold using small, evenly spaced stitches worked at right angles to the gold.

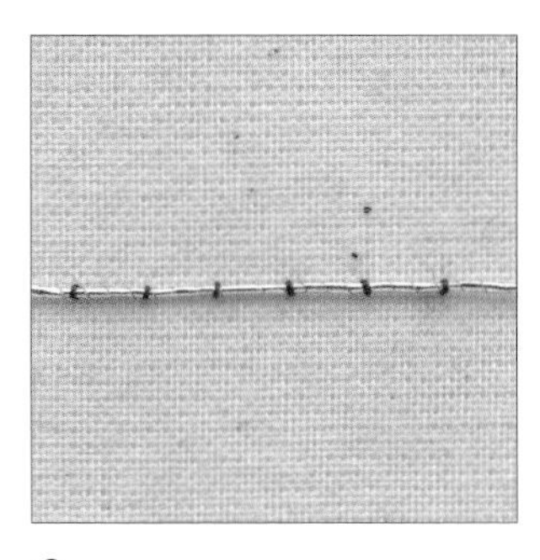

3 Continue stitching in this way until the desired length has been achieved. Finish off the sewing thread at the end.

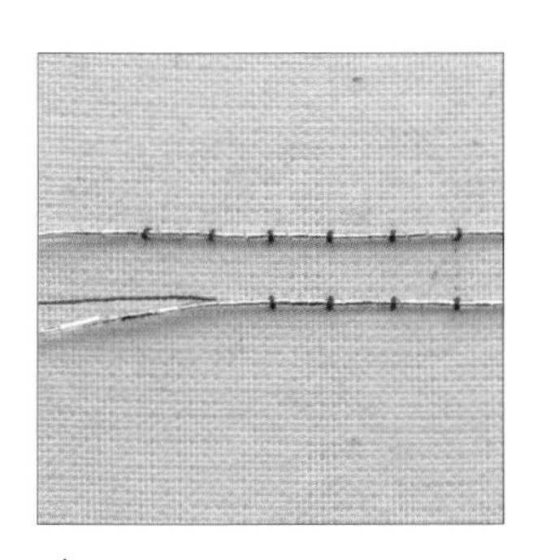

4 Lay a second strand of gold thread alongside the first and stitch it down in the same way, placing the stitches parallel with the first set.

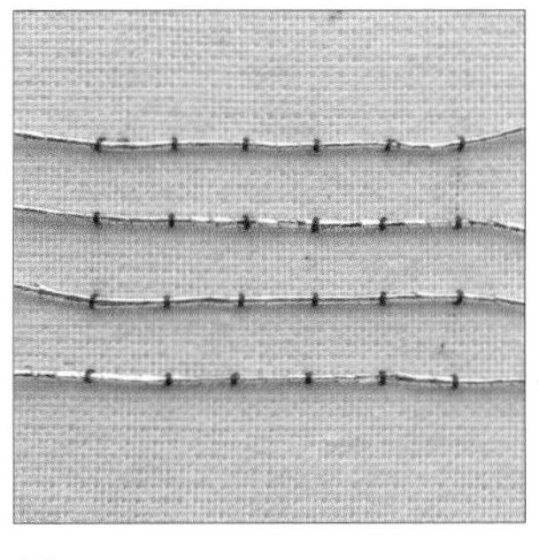

5 Stitch on more lines of gold until you have the required number, spacing them evenly.

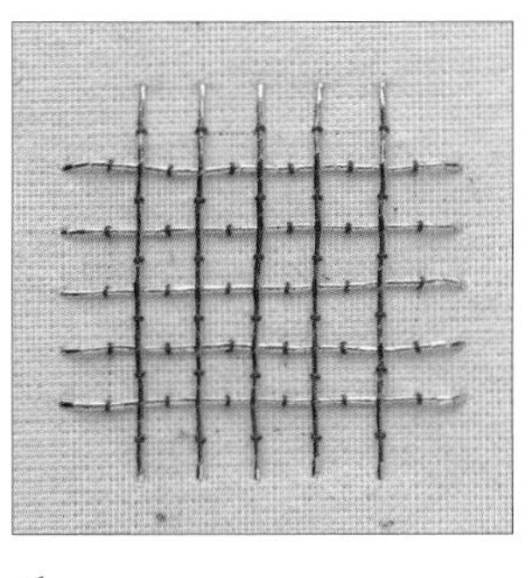

6 Lay more strands at 90° to the first, placing them in between the stitches on the vertical lines. Stitch these down in the same way, placing the stitches in between the vertical lines of gold.

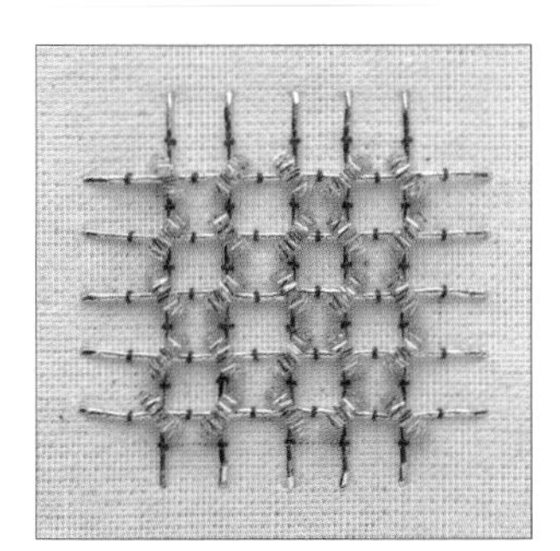

7 Decorate the trellis, for example by stitching purls across the intersections as shown here.

USING COLOUR

Metal threads are, of course, beautiful, but when you add colour the lustre of the metal is given another dimension and depth. There are a number of ways in which to do this, including overstretched pearl purl (page 52) and using a coloured thread to create a pattern as shown with the Elizabethan twist threads (page 54). This section shows you how to create diaper or trellis couching, how to draw a pattern on to your base fabric and then go over it in thread, and Or Nué, which is a technique in which you can fill a whole area with gold held down with coloured threads or break it up by interspersing it with painted areas. Colour and gold is a very versatile technique and can be experimented with extensively.

Still Waters Flow

Helen McCook

This piece includes an example of cutwork over soft string, spangles, beads, pearl purl, overstretched pearl purl with a coloured core, twist, silver passing thread with coloured bricking, s-ing, kid and patterned couching. A close-up of the central section is shown on page 62.

DIAPER COUCHING

Begin by drawing your design on to the background fabric. The lines represent where the couching stitches are to be placed and at what angle. In the pattern opposite, stitches that fall on the diagonals are worked at 45° to the gold, and those on the verticals are worked at 90° to the gold. Stitches that fall in between the lines are worked in a self-coloured thread and are therefore invisible; those on the lines are worked in a coloured thread.

1 Take two strands of metal thread (here I have used silver) and lay them down one side of the shape. Thread two needles – one with a single strand of self-coloured thread and the other with two strands of pink six-stranded cotton. Work a single holding stitch using the self-coloured thread at the top of the shape, then work a diagonal couching stitch on the first diagonal line using the pink thread.

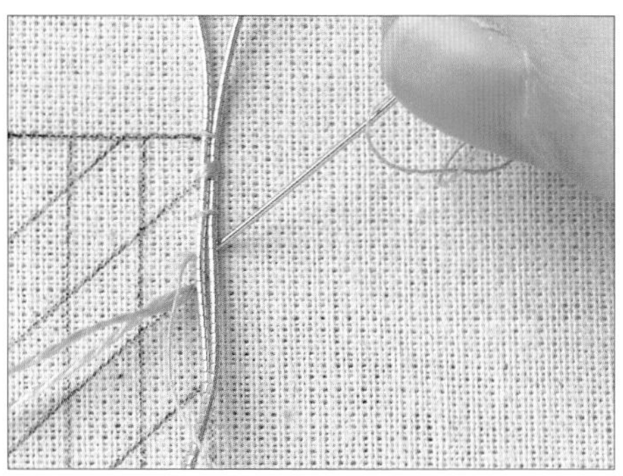

2 Continue to couch down the silver threads, placing a regular number of horizontal holding stitches in between the diagonal pink couching stitches.

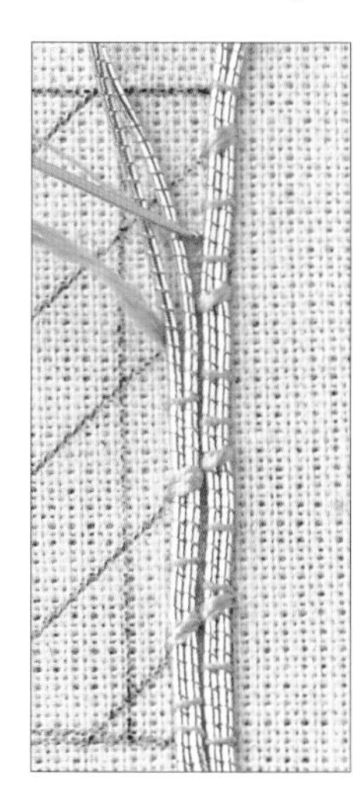

3 When you reach the bottom of the shape, lay another pair of silver threads alongside the first and couch back up to the top of the shape in the same way. Work the holding stitches in between those in the previous row to create a brick pattern.

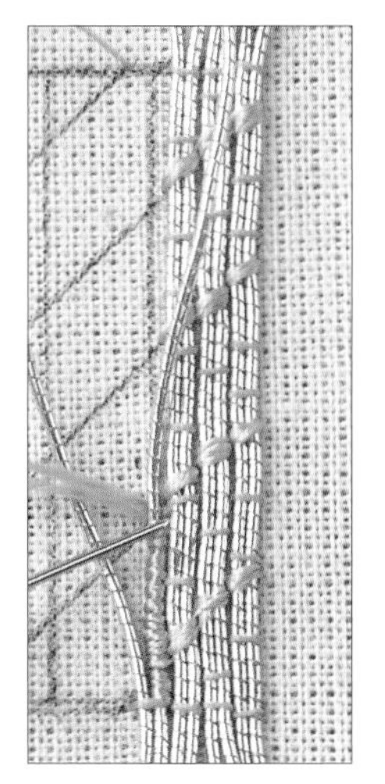

4 Continue across the shape to the first vertical line. Here, place a holding stitch over two silver threads, as before. Couch down only the right-hand thread on the line using the pink thread and closely worked, horizontal couching stitches.

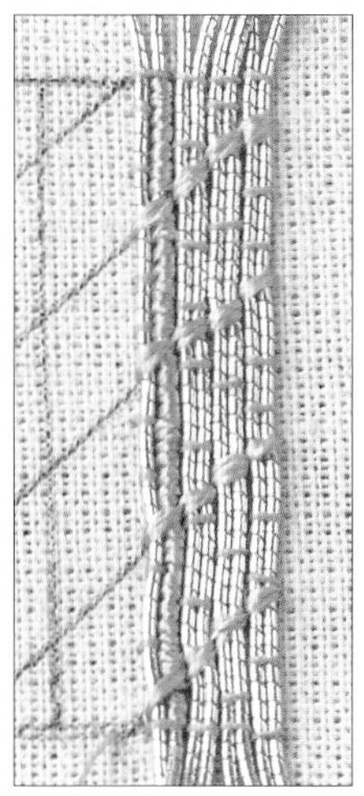

5 When you reach a diagonal, work a single, diagonal couching stitch over both silver threads. Work to the top of the shape. Secure both silver threads with self-coloured holding stitches.

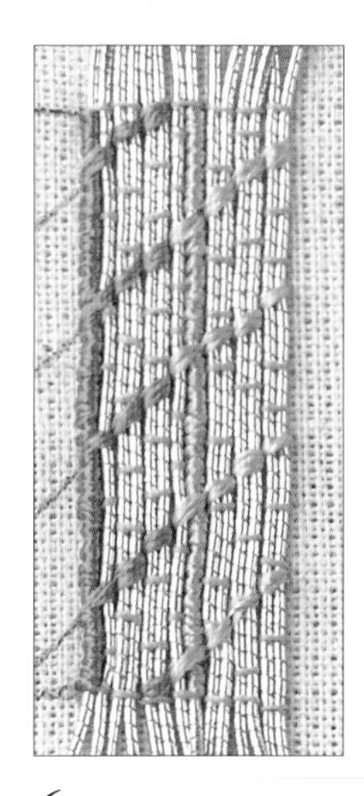

6 Work the next vertical block in the same way as the first, using a different coloured thread. To finish, take all the sewing threads through to the back, plunge the metal and fasten off.

OR NUÉ

Begin by drawing your design on to fabric and choose your thread colours, then thread two needles – one with a self-coloured thread and one with a contrasting thread. If you are using more than one contrasting colour, start with the first one that you will be using in the design. You will start from the top of the design and work downwards.

Early twentieth-century Or Nué training piece depicting angels, worked by RSN students and left unfinished for training purposes. Silk shading and Or Nué on linen. (RSN Collection 96)

1 Cut a length of Japanese gold that is about twice the width of your design plus 8cm (3in), fold it in half and lay it across the top of the design with the loop level with the left-hand side. Secure the loop with a stitch in the self-coloured thread. Continue to couch down the two threads, changing to the coloured thread where required.

Note

If you are working individual strands of Japanese thread or do not mind a slightly bulkier turn, then you could turn the ends and work the whole piece with the same metal thread and only plunge at the start and finish of the piece. This is something to consider at the design stage.

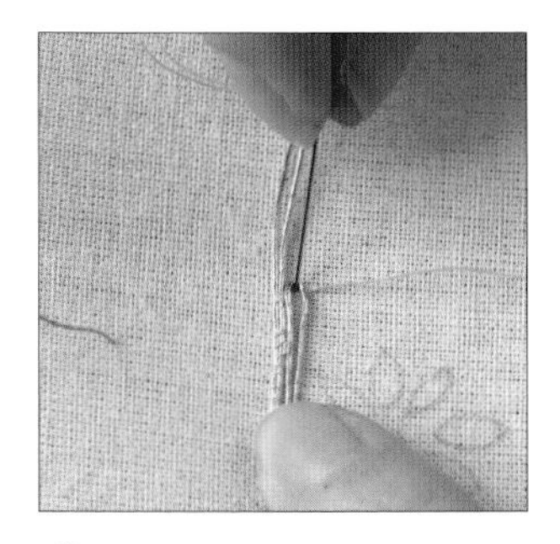

2 Start the next piece of metal thread at the opposite end to where you started on the first row. Start the thread in the same way, ensuring that the gold will sit close to the previous row with no visible gaps.

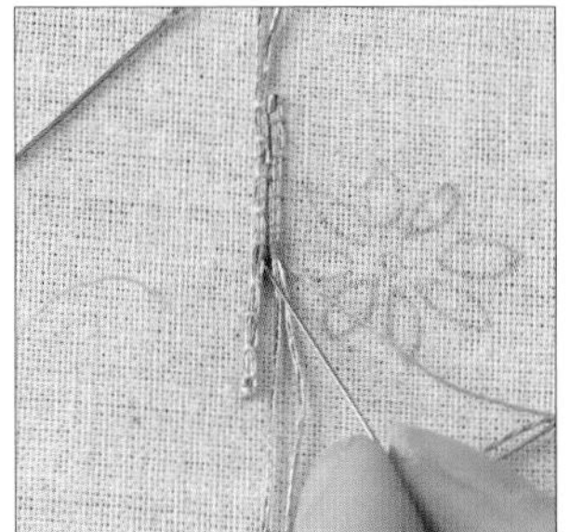

3 Work your way along the gold as before, placing couching stitches in self-coloured thread where you wish the stitches to be invisible, and changing to the coloured thread and working close stitches where colour is required.

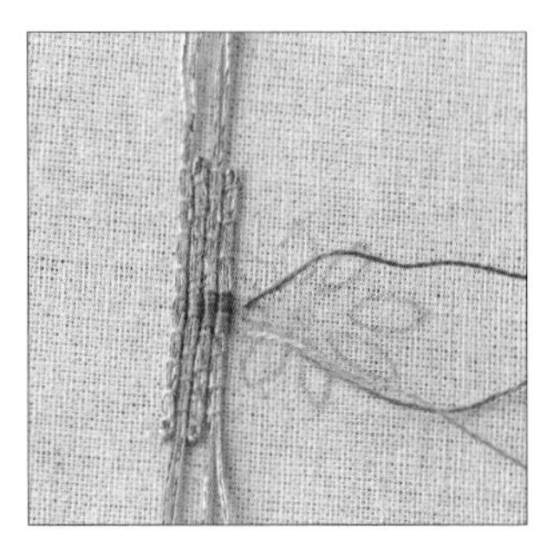

4 As you progress back and forth across the design, introduce more contrasting colours as demanded by the design. Work the coloured stitches close together for solid areas of colour; space them out for a more subtle effect.

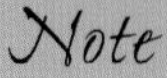

Ensure that you come up on the outer edge of each new piece of gold and take the needle down into the fabric on the edge which is against the previous row of gold (in the same way that you would for normal couching).

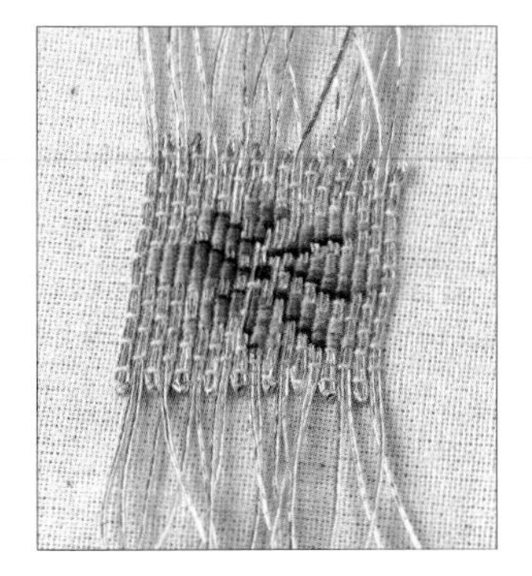

The completed design.

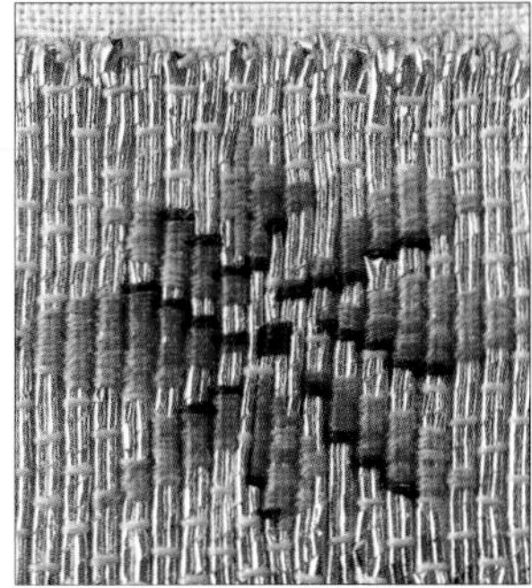

The completed design with the ends plunged.

OR NUÉ WITH PAINT

There are two approaches to working Or Nué over a painted background: either fill the entire background with colour and use it as guidance only for the colour of the stitching; or leave some areas of the background unpainted and stitch only in these areas, leaving the coloured areas unstitched. Watercolour, fabric or silk paints are suitable mediums for colouring the fabric.

Creating blocks of strong colour

In the first example below, a strong surface pattern is created by couching down pairs of gold threads using a contrasting thread. The pattern is painted on to the background fabric and provides a guide for the placement of the coloured couching stitches.

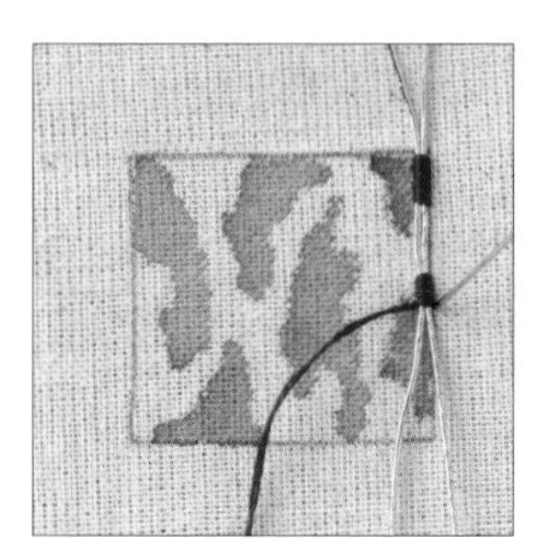

1 Take two strands of Japanese gold and lay them down one side of the coloured shape (see page 81). With two strands of six-stranded cotton/mouline thread in an aesthetically pleasing colour, couch down the gold using closely worked stitches with no gaps in between. Stitch with the coloured thread only where the background is painted; where the background is unpainted, secure the gold by couching in a brickwork pattern using a self-coloured thread.

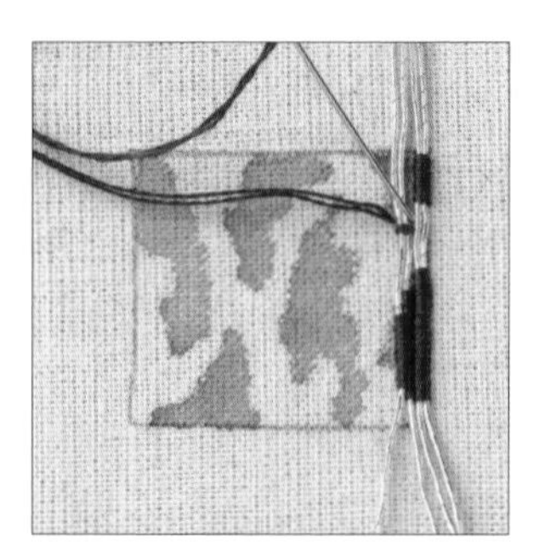

2 Couch down the second pair of gold threads in the same way, working from the bottom of the shape to the top.

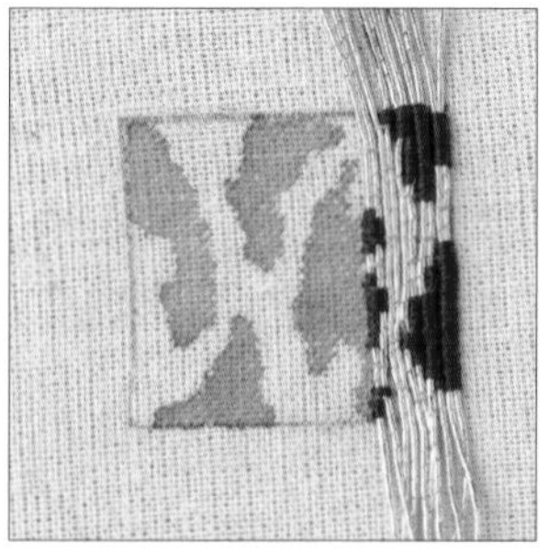

3 Continue working in this way across the shape.

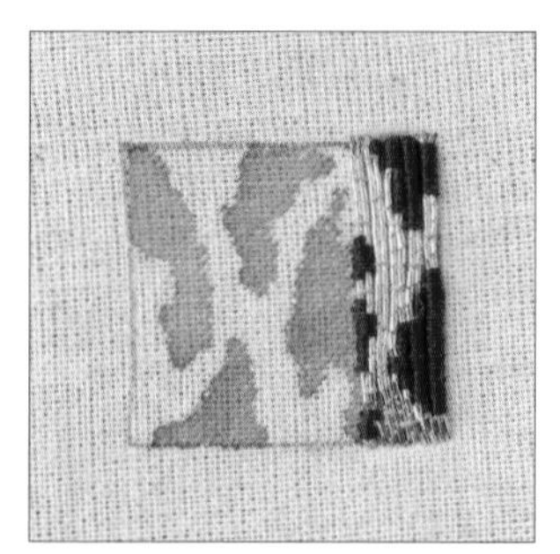

4 To finish, take all the sewing threads through to the back, plunge the gold and fasten off (see page 47).

Creating a random effect with two colours

Here, a more irregular pattern has been created using randomly spaced stitches and two different coloured threads.

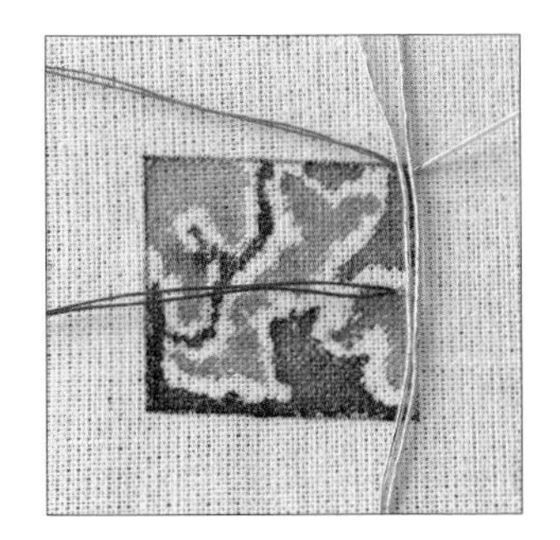

1 Begin by laying a pair of Japanese gold threads down one side of the coloured shape. Thread two strands of six-stranded cotton in two different colours into separate needles. Bring each thread through to the front where you intend to start stitching in that colour. Place the first couching stitch at the top of the shape.

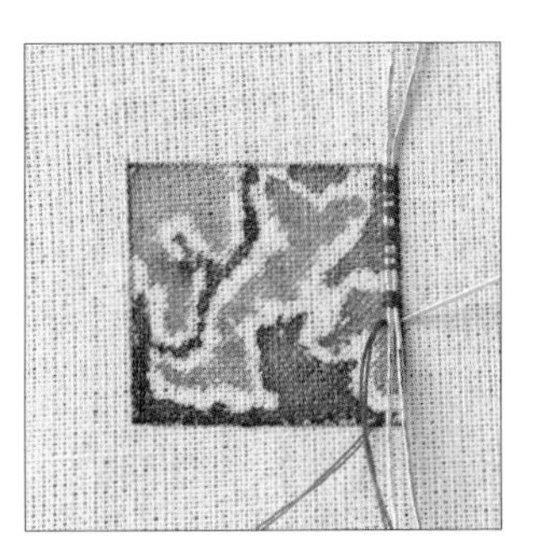

2 Work from the top to the bottom of the shape, stitching only within the coloured areas. Use randomly spaced stitches so that the gold shows through. Take the gold across the uncoloured shapes, securing it using one or two stitches worked in a self-coloured thread only where the gap is large.

3 Continue working in this way across the shape.

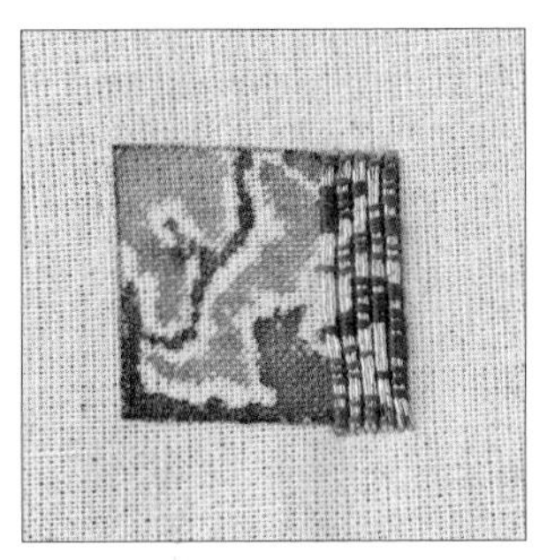

4 To finish, take all the sewing threads through to the back, plunge the gold and fasten off (see page 47).

Note

If crossing a large unpainted area, hold the gold in place with one or more stitches worked in a self-coloured thread.

Creating subtle shading effects

In the example below, the thread colour is varied to reflect changes in the colour of the background. Gaps are left between the lines of gold so that the background is still visible, creating a subtle play of colour and light.

1 Take a single strand of Japanese gold and lay it across one side of a coloured shape. Choose a six-stranded cotton thread that matches the colour of the background at the start of the gold thread. Using two strands of your chosen cotton, couch down the gold using small, evenly spaced stitches.

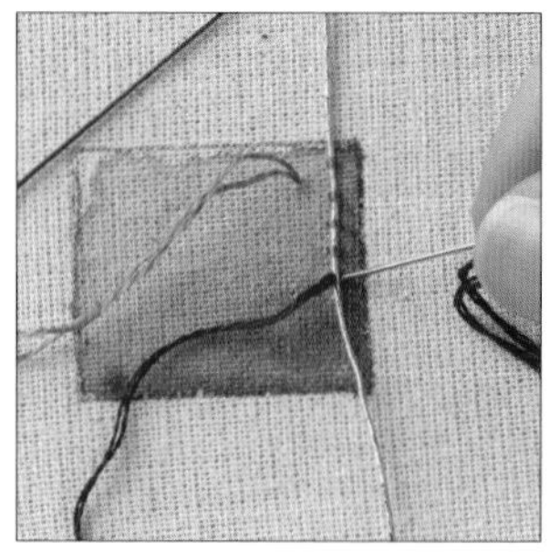

2 Change to a different thread to reflect the change in the background colour. Leave the first thread on the needle and use a new needle for the new thread. Bring the first colour through to the front of the fabric ready to resume stitching – to the left of the first row, halfway between the first two stitches.

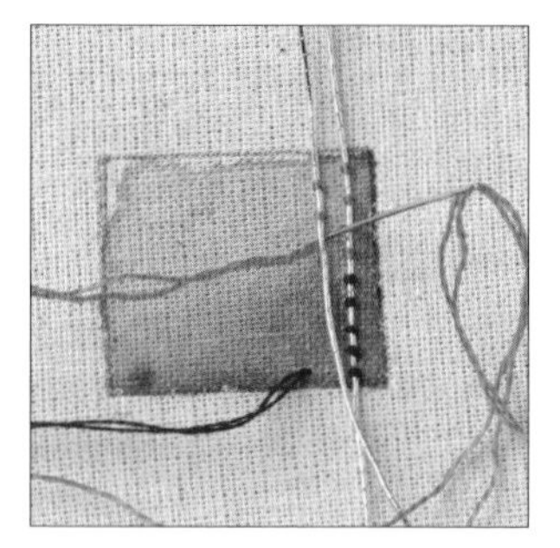

3 Stitch to the end of the gold in the second colour, then lay a second gold strand down alongside the first, leaving a small gap in between. Position the second colour to the left of the new strand, halfway between the last two stitches, and resume stitching in the first colour at the top of the new strand. Place the stitches in between those in the first row.

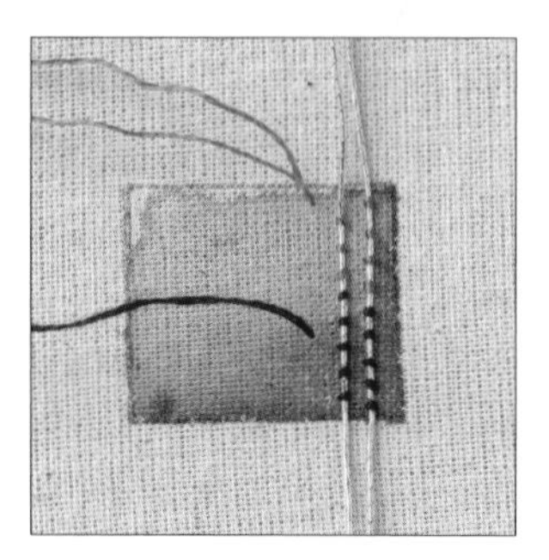

4 Continue stitching in this pattern, changing from one colour to the other to reflect the changes in the background.

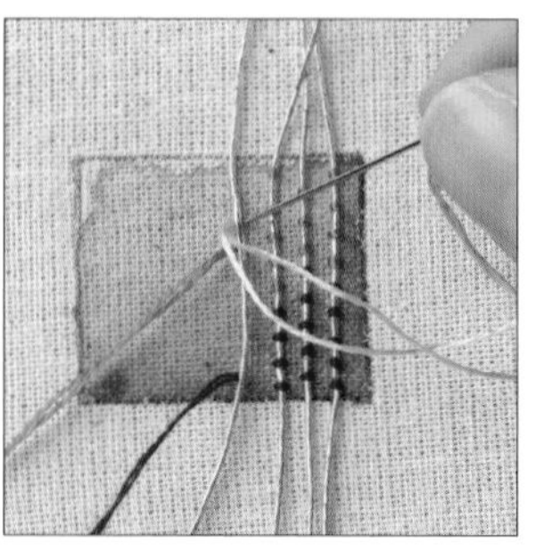

5 Introduce further colours for a more subtle effect. Use a different needle for each thread.

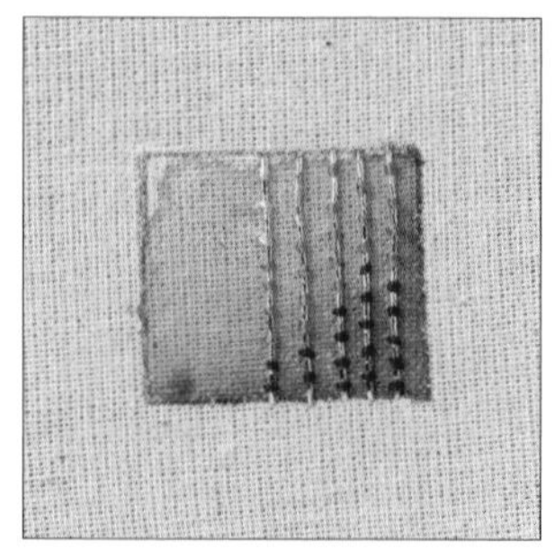

6 To finish, take all the sewing threads through to the back, plunge the gold and fasten off.

In the example below, this technique has been applied on a larger scale to achieve a highly contemporary design that uses traditional goldwork techniques to achieve a more painterly effect.

1 Draw on the design with Indian ink permanent marker and paint it with watercolour.

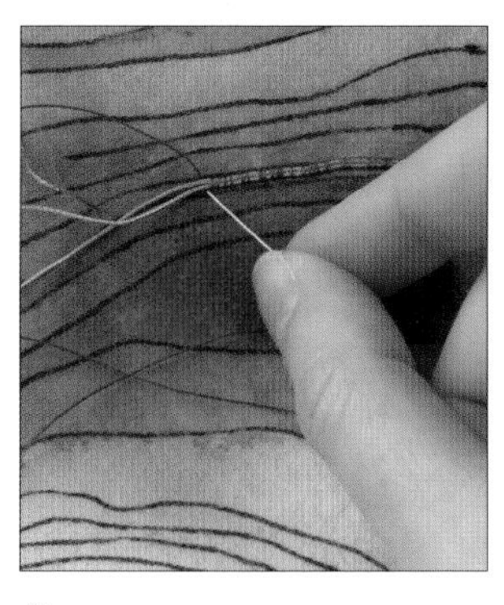

2 Lay a pair of silver threads along one of the contours and couch it down using a coloured cotton thread. Use randomly spaced stitches, varying the spacing depending on the intensity of colour you wish to achieve.

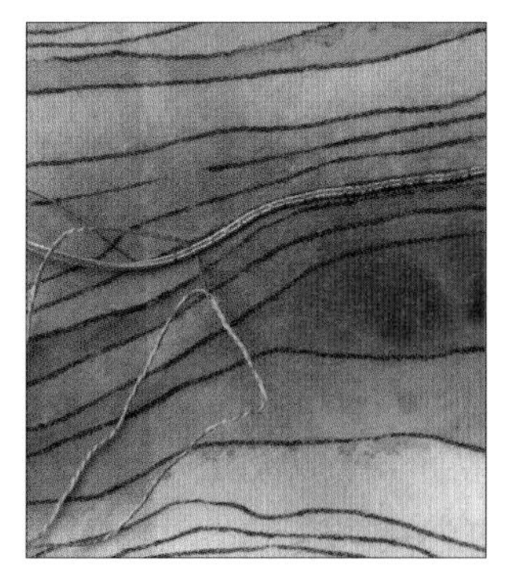

3 Vary the thread colour to match the background, using a different needle for each colour. Mark the points along the line at which the colour changes by bringing through threads in the appropriate colour.

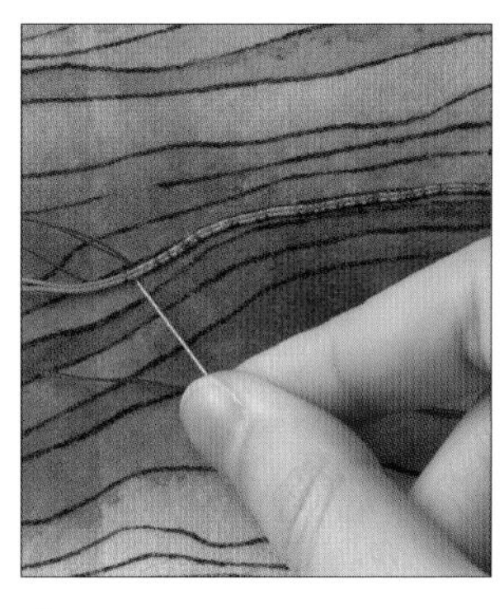

4 When you change colour, work stitches in the second colour between the stitches worked in the first colour to achieve a blending effect.

COMBINING TECHNIQUES

This section is an opportunity to show you a few finished embroideries, with close-up images, in order to illustrate how the different techniques which have been described in previous sections of the book may be worked together, and hopefully to help inspire you to develop your own ideas. Remember that these are just a few options and the techniques can be mixed and matched to suit your design.

Ageing Acanthus *(detail)*
Spangles, surface stitching and couching.

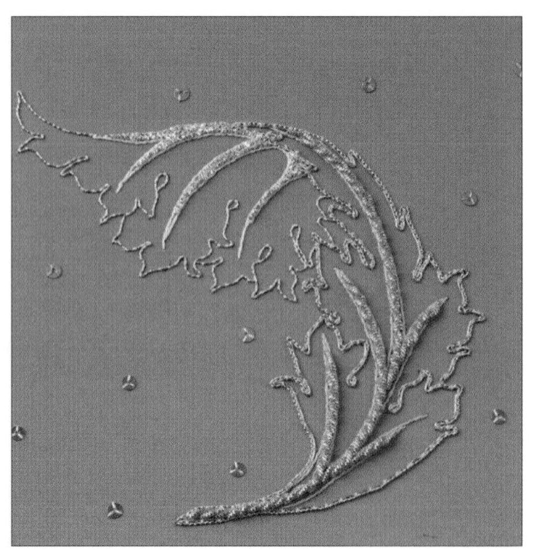

Ageing Acanthus *(detail)*
Spangles, cutwork and couching.

THREE WISHES

By Helen McCook.

Finished size: 48 x 25cm (19 x 9¾in).

If you ever play the three wishes game with friends, you will notice that the first dream wish is often very simple, the second dream wish is a little bigger and more complex and the third wish often expands into a grandiose and intricate story. It was this expansion and growth from small and simple to large and complex and the hidden depths that these dreams reveal in your friends and loved ones that inspired this embroidered panel, which shows three differently sized stars with intertwining shooting tails and flashes.

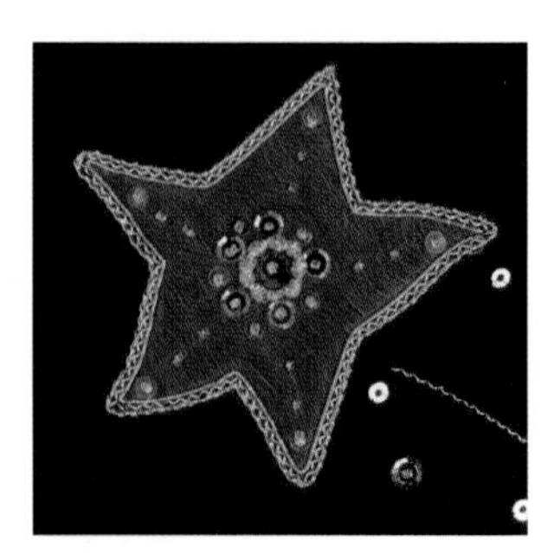

Wish One.

Materials

Silver, gold and copper metal threads, including rococco, Japanese, pearl purl, bright check, organza appliqué, spangles and crystals, worked on a mole-grey velvet ground fabric.

Techniques

Overstretched pearl purl, spangles with single stitches and chips, crystals with chips, couching, cutwork, bright check chips and appliqué.

Having designed the composition, I framed up and transferred the design to the fabric. I then worked the appliqué, followed by couching, pearl purl, chips, crystals and spangles.

Wish Two.

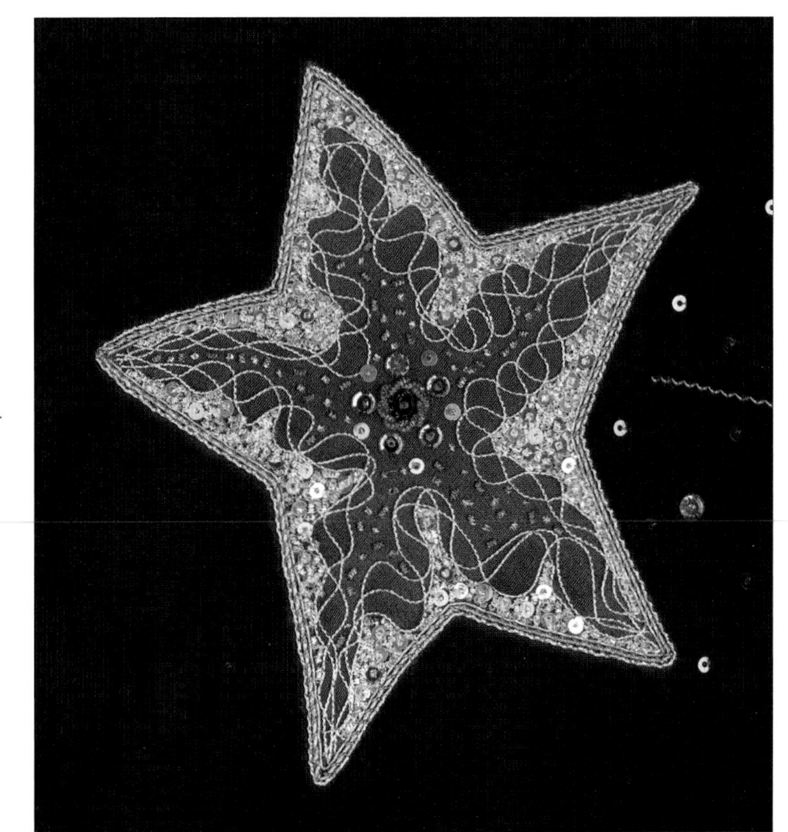

Wish Three.

INDIAN SUMMER

By Helen McCook.

Finished size: 10 x 15cm (4 x 6in).

Having been born and raised in Birmingham, I've learnt to appreciate the vibrancy of colour and culture all around me. As such, I wanted to pay a small homage to that by looking at hot, spicy Indian silk fabrics and creating a design which was a little reminiscent of the traditional *mehndi* patterns with their delicacy and happy associations.

Hot, spicy orange and azure blue silks are balanced with a mixture of golden threads and orange metallic thread in a scrolling floral design.

Materials

Gilt smooth purl and bright check, pearl purl, Japanese, rococco, coloured metallic twist, spangles, sequins and seed beads applied to a silk ground.

Techniques

Pearl purl, spangles with chips, sequins with beads, couching, cutwork over soft string, bright check chips, beadwork and appliqué.

I carefully transferred the design on to the silk using a light box and then put the fabric into a ring frame, ensuring that the tension was nice and tight all round. I worked the soft-string padding and executed the appliqué areas. I then embroidered down all of the couched threads, plunged their ends and fastened them neatly and securely at the back of the piece. Next came the pearl purl and chips, followed by sequins, spangles and beadwork. Last to be worked was the area of cutwork over soft string.

The finished piece (shown above right; also shown on page 1) and the initial colour drawing.

SPRING FLIGHT

By Helen McCook.

Finished size: 30 x 35cm (11¾ x 13¾in).

This piece is a celebration of new beginnings and renewal. Every year, the blossom bursts forth and the birds return from their winter retreats, and with them come fresh colour, warmer weather and hopeful, happier attitudes. Every spring offers a turning point; longer, lighter days and new life. This piece embodies that celebration for me.

This piece combines a delicate balance of heavily worked areas with finely wrought, open areas utilising a mixture of cherry blossom reds and pinks with the bronze, copper, gold, silver and blue contrast of the bird in flight.

Materials

Silver, gilt, copper and bronze fine passing threads, copper, gilt, silver, pink and red rough purl, silver, gilt and copper bright check, silver and gilt spangles, gilt pearl purl, gilt and coloured metallic twist, seed beads and sequins to Eau de Nil silk ground.

Techniques

Couching, cutwork, s-ing with spangles, chips, and overstretched pearl purl.

I stretched my fabric into a slate frame and then carefully transferred the design on to the silk using the prick-and-pounce method. I then worked the carpet-felt padding and craft-felt padding, followed by the couching threads and pearl purl. The next stage to be worked was the chipping, sequins, spangles and beadwork, followed by the cutwork to the wings, tail, beak and flowers.

Below left: the complete embroidery; below right: detail (see also page 37 and the front cover).

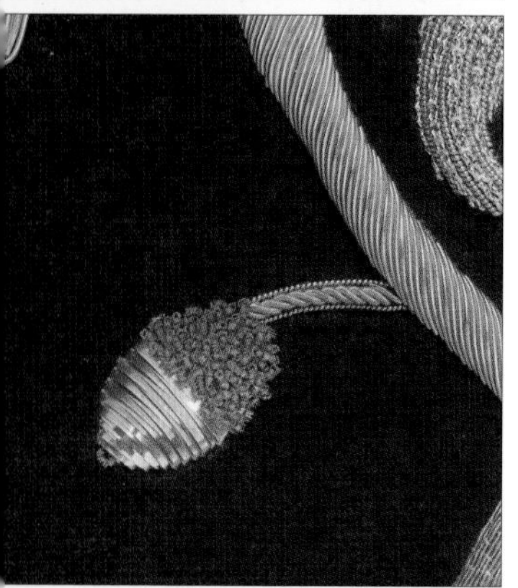
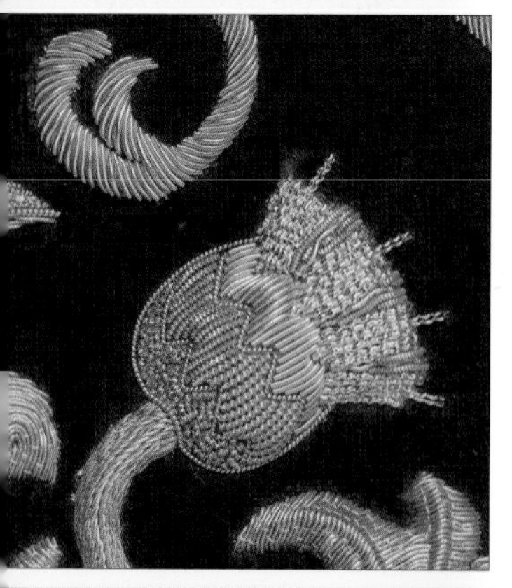
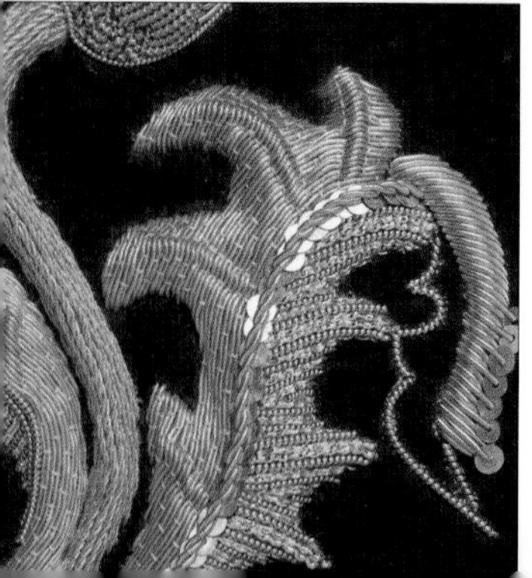

MORE A SCOTTISH THISTLE THAN AN ENGLISH ROSE

By Helen McCook.

Finished size: 71 x 68.5cm (28 x 27in).

This piece was worked while I was in my second year as an apprentice at the RSN in 2002. The requirement was to take inspiration from Coronation robes from the past and create a new design. Mine was quite a personal response based upon my Scottish heritage (represented by the thistle) but also showing reference to the fact that I was born and raised in England, which is represented by the acorn and rose leaves. The five laurel leaves on the right-hand stem symbolise the five members of my family and the stems intertwine and curl towards each other to show that we are all a product of our environment and culture. The leaves face outwards to represent the space that is essential for every individual in a family so that there is room for them to grow and follow their own path.

Materials

Assorted gilt and gold metal threads including plate, rococco, twist, Japanese thread, passing, gimp, bullion, spangles, pearl purl, smooth purl, rough purl, bright check threads and dull/wire check threads, worked on a dark blue velvet ground.

Techniques

The techniques employed across the piece are very traditional and include couching, couching over hard string, pearl purl, chips, cutwork over soft string, cutwork over carpet felt, s-ing, s-ing with spangles, plate over felt, chips and looped chips.

Having framed up the calico and velvet in a slate frame I pricked, pounced and carefully painted the design on to the fabric to ensure I had a fine, even line. I then applied the carpet-felt padding, craft-felt padding, soft-string padding and hard-string padding. All areas of couching were then embroidered, and had their ends plunged and neatly secured at the back of the fabric. I then worked all areas of pearl purl, followed by the chips. The gimp was then applied and the plate was stitched down. All areas of cutwork were then completed.

Above: the complete embroidery.

Left: details, from top to bottom: rough, smooth, dull check and bright check purls over soft-string padding with s-ing detailing; rough and smooth purls over soft string, looped chips and plate over felt, and combination couching over craft-felt and carpet-felt padding; rough and smooth purls over soft-string padding, couching over hard string, combination couching over carpet-felt and craft-felt padding, rough, smooth, dull check and bright check purls, and chips over carpet felt and craft felt with a pearl purl edge; combination couching and couching over hard string, carpet felt and craft felt with pearl purl and s-ing with spangles, cutwork with spangles, pearl purl and cutwork over soft string and carpet and craft felt.

POMEGRANATE AND GILLY FLOWER

By Helen McCook.

Finished size: 15 x 16cm (6 x 6¼in).

This piece derives its inspiration from the Elizabethan and Stuart floral designs that were so often translated on to items of clothing and accessories in embroidery, and also from the texture and pattern of Jacobean embroidery.

I hoped to create a robust but feminine floral design with areas of varying texture and colour, and with bursts of rich colour to delight the eye in the same way that the original embroideries did, and still do today.

Materials

Seed beads, sequins, fine copper mesh, copper bright check, coloured rough purl, stranded cotton, rococco, coloured metallic twist, gilt Japanese thread and fine silver passing thread.

Techniques

Chain stitch, straight stitch, stem stitch, metal mesh appliqué, trellis with looped chip decoration, couching, overstretched pearl purl with coloured core, feather stitch in coloured rough purl, sequins with bead centres and beads.

I carefully transferred the design on to the fabric using a light box and then placed the fabric into a ring frame, ensuring that the fabric was taut and stretched evenly. As the first stage for the embroidery, I worked all of the areas of surface stitching using stranded cottons, followed by the couching and pearl purl. All sequins, copper mesh, beads and chips were then applied, followed by the cutwork. In the case of the pomegranate stem, the beads were worked at the same time as the cutwork, as they need to be worked in order.

The finished piece (shown on the facing page) was based on my initial colour drawing above. An enlarged section of this piece is shown on page 73.

SNOWDROPS

By Helen McCook.

Finished size: 17 x 18cm (6¾ x 7in).

This embroidered piece is inspired by a stone carving from Iona Abbey. I was intrigued by the balance which had been struck through the use of hard stone skilfully carved to render a delicate vision of snowdrops and the hope that the first flowers of spring offer after the harshness of winter. I felt that I would like to explore these parallels by creating an embroidery in metal, which is generally also equated to hard, cold and unyielding qualities.

The snowdrops are intertwined to allow for positive and negative space, and there are flashes of colour and delicate shading throughout the piece that have been explored by the use of beads, diamanté, coloured metallic twist and assorted shades of stranded cotton.

Materials

Japanese thread, spangles, pearl purl, twist, smooth purl, bright check, seed beads, diamanté, stranded cotton on to a soft blue-grey silk dupion ground.

Techniques

Couching, fish-scale spangles with French knot centres, chips, cutwork, beading and application of diamanté.

The design was carefully transferred on to the fabric, which was then stretched tight in a ring frame. All of the areas of couching were worked first, followed by the pearl purl. Next came the chips, diamanté, beadwork, spangles and their French knots. The last technique applied to the design was the cutwork.

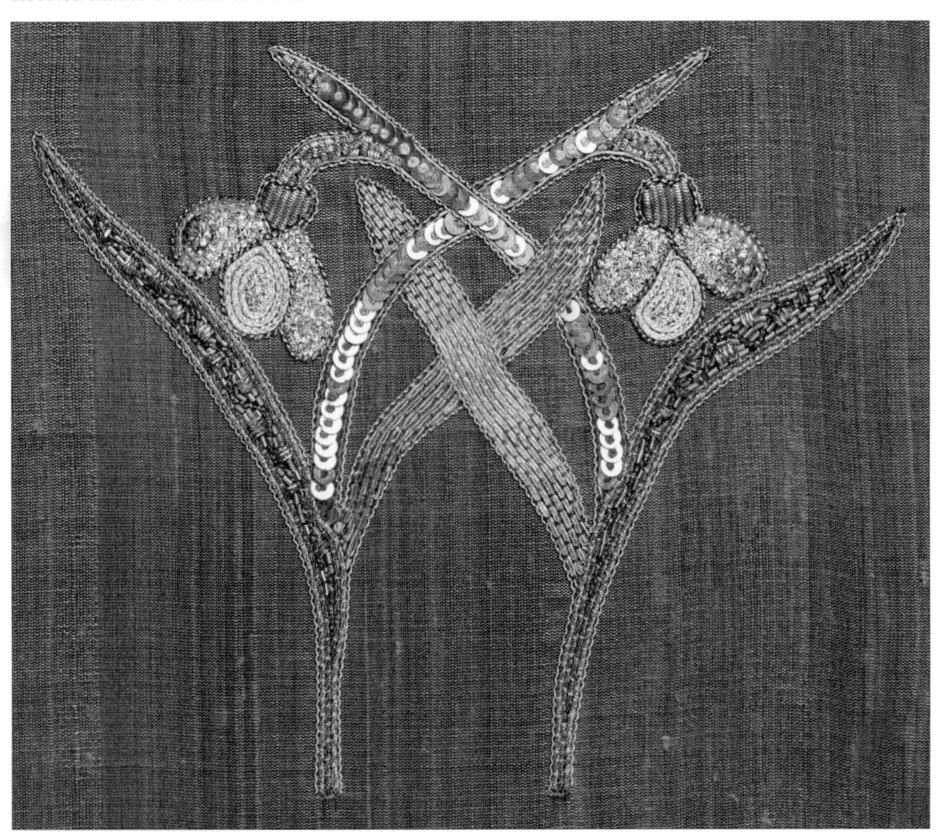

I developed this embroidery (shown on the facing page) from a simple pencil drawing (left) to which I added the stitches I wished to use. To this I later added colour (below). An enlarged section of this embroidery is shown on page 44.

INDEX